## VOICES OF SOME INDIVIDUALS YOU WILL MEET IN *A SEMINARY DEAN'S EXPERIMENT WITH SERVANT LEADERSHIP*

It remains in my mind as one of those flashbulb memories, which to this day I can vividly recall, when Dr. Thomson Mathew, who at the time was the Associate Dean of the Graduate School of Theology and Ministry at Oral Roberts University, called to ask if I would consider joining their faculty as an Assistant Professor of Counseling. It was a phone call that changed my life. Soon after accepting his invitation, he became the Dean of the entire College of Theology and Ministry, and I had the privilege of working under his leadership for 16 years until he transitioned in 2016.

During those 16 years the seminary encountered significant challenges and changes, but Dr. Mathew's guidance and steady hand enabled us to successfully traverse those troubled waters. He created an environment of stability and safety, which allowed us to find the support we needed, often through very honest yet caring conversations, so that we could persevere and even thrive. The University, and especially the College of Theology and Ministry, owe him a debt of gratitude. He led with integrity and compassion, earning our loyalty and respect.

As a colleague Dr. Mathew became a trusted friend and advisor. I valued his wisdom and insight, which was often gleaned over many a lunchroom conversation. I miss those spirited discussions where a diverse group of faculty would gather each day and visit about whatever was on their minds. Topics ranged from theology to politics, and our perspectives from conservative to liberal, but I will always treasure the collegiality with which we addressed the issues and each other. We shared a common bond in the Spirit that kept us united. Due in large part to Dr. Mathew's leadership, we felt like family and when he decided it was time to leave the Dean's position, it created a sense of a loss that is still deeply felt even years later.

I am honored to endorse Dr. Mathew's book on leadership lessons learned as a seminary Dean. I believe that his deep understanding and astute perception will be of great help to both current and future generations of leaders. As a beneficiary of his guidance and example, and in stepping into his former role as Associate Dean of the College of Theology and Ministry, I can honestly say that I am standing on the shoulders of a giant.

**Bill Buker, DMin, PhD, LPC, Associate Dean and Senior Professor of Professional Counseling, College of Theology and Ministry, Oral Roberts University**

In fall 1999, while I was chair of the undergraduate theology department, Dr. Thomson K. Mathew, then associate dean of the seminary, asked if I would consider moving to the graduate theology school to assume Dr. Howard Ervin's position and become the Old Testament professor in the seminary. Ervin, one of my revered professors as a student in the seminary, was planning to retire; however, he chose to remain. The Lord had other plans. When Mathew was appointed dean in the spring 2000 semester, he again extended an invitation to me, this time to join the administrative team as the associate dean of the seminary. I felt the Lord's leading to embrace this call to serve. The Lord had already been preparing my heart for a change. Mathew prayerfully extended invitations to other qualified individuals and formed an outstanding administrative team.

Through the years of working with Mathew, I can attest to the fact that he has followed Jesus' example of Spirit-led servant leadership. He did not aspire for positions and titles. He desired to be God's servant and serve others. An example of Mathew's servant leadership approach occurred when he became dean of the College of Theology and Ministry (COTM). Mathew was given the opportunity to move to his $6^{th}$ floor office, the floor where executive offices were located, and lead the COTM from there. He chose to remain on the $4^{th}$ floor where the seminary was located because he wanted to be available to his administrative team, faculty, and students. He maintained an open-door policy and used the $6^{th}$ floor office for special meetings and times of prayer. Prayer was always an integral part of his leadership.

Mathew has been, and continues to be, a trustworthy and transparent leader. He built a strong and competent administrative team. He kept them informed, cast vision, identified their gifts, involved them in decision-making, listened to their counsel, empowered them to accomplish their respective responsibilities, provided them with resources, extended to them wise pastoral counsel, and advocated for them. Throughout the time of his leadership of the COTM, Mathew promoted an atmosphere of camaraderie and family among the members of the team.

Mathew is an outstanding example of a Spirit-led servant of God with an impeccable character. He is a man of faith and integrity and adheres to strong Christian ethical and moral values. He is also a devoted husband, father, grandfather, colleague and friend, and a conference speaker at home and abroad. From my perspective as a colleague, I would apply Paul's words to Mathew in reference to his personal life, ministry, and the powerful legacy he has forged through the years: "Follow my example, as I follow the example of Christ" (1 Cor. 11:1 NIV).

Over the years, Mathew has demonstrated that he is a Spirit-led leader and minister of the Gospel of Jesus Christ. Even after his retirement from ORU, he continues to train future generations of Spirit-led leaders and ministers through his teaching, ministry, and books. One highlight of my teaching and ministry was joining the Mathews in Bangalore, India, in the summer of 2019. Mathew taught the first Doctor of Ministry course at New Life College, and I taught the second course. I thank the Lord for the relationship I have had with Dr. Thomson K. Mathew, his wife Molly, and his family. They have embraced me, and my husband Randy, as part of their extended family. Randy and I treasure this friendship as a gift from the Lord.

**Cheryl L. Iverson, PhD, Professor Emeritus and Former Associate Dean, College of Theology and Ministry, Oral Roberts University**

I have had the great honor to have worked intimately with many Godly men over the 50 years of my ministry, but none as intimately or for as long as Dr. Thomson Mathew. I served with him for 28 years. He was my friend, my colleague, my boss, and, although I am older than he in some ways, he was a mentor.

Under his leadership we imagined what theological education might look like in the 21$^{st}$ century. We designed new programs for professional ministry and new delivery systems for the new constituencies. We found ways to assess and measure the curricular success of amorphous tasks like that originally given to Oral Roberts, "raise up my students to hear God's voice." We survived and thrived during several changes in leadership, and throughout those changing times we were protected from the vagaries of the academy. Dr. Mathew molded us from a group of individuals with disparate tasks, although working in the same arena, to a unified group of colleagues, sisters and brothers all working for the same goal: the education and formation of men and women for Christian ministry.

Although I know it was his way of working with all of the seminary faculty because he made all of us feel this way—we were part of his family—he made me feel as though I was uniquely important to him and needed. He was *always* available, listened (his pastoral care skills were evident), spoke, and acted wisely.

On one occasion I was frustrated about something, probably having to do with how I saw things so differently than my colleagues, and I went to him to tell him of my frustration. He listened as he always did and then he responded. "Decker," he said, he always called me Decker, "you are a missionary." I was disarmed by his comment, but it struck a chord deep within me because my parents were missionaries. I knew what he meant. He had an ability to speak to the deepest motivations of each of us, calling forth the best of us in service to God.

**Edward E. Decker, Jr., PhD, Former Professor of Christian Counseling and Director of the MA in Christian Counseling Program**

The Korean language DMin program at ORU was launched in 1992 and terminated in 2012. During this period, 138 pastors from Korea earned their DMin degrees. They were trained for advanced level ministry through whole person education with the power of the Holy Spirit and a focus on healing. The following data demonstrates how these graduates are impacting life and ministry in Korea. The breakdown of graduates by denominations:

    Methodist Church – 47 pastors
    Presbyterian Church – 33 pastors
    Full Gospel Church – 30 pastors
    Evangelical Holiness Church – 13 pastors
    Foursquare Gospel Church – 8 pastors
    Baptist Church – 4 pastors
    Nazarene Church – 3 pastors

Of the DMin graduates, six served as denominational presidents, five serve as bishops in the Methodist Church, seven serve as chairpersons of Boards of Trustees of Colleges and Universities, seventeen serve as faculty members, five serve as Presidents or Deans of Universities and Bible Colleges, 13 serve as missionaries, and five are leading Christian organizations such as Pentateuch Research Center, Prayer Mountain, and Healing Center. ORU graduates have served the Korean Church especially in the area of whole person healing. They led 16 Healing Crusades at Dr. Yonggi Cho's Prayer Mountain, and several more at other prayer mountains. Currently seven graduates are serving the Korean Church as healing evangelists.

I first met Dr. Mathew at the City of Faith Hospital in 1989 when he served as a hospital chaplain. So I have known him for more than 33 years now. I was much influenced by his life, faith, and teachings. I can summarize our relationship and my observations about him as follows.

He is a student of the Bible. This is evident in his sermons. Whenever he preaches, his messages are fresh and challenging, reflecting his prayerful study of the word of God. Even though he was leading a big seminary, he was primarily a man of God and a student of His word.

He is an educator. Dr. Mathew not only taught the DMin students on the ORU campus, but he also visited Korea more than 10 times. Whenever he visited, he taught the seminary students at Asia LIFE University (ALU) where I served as President. Students loved his teaching and asked me to invite him more often because he loved the students and provided outstanding teaching. His teachings were new because he studied his major areas continually even when he worked as an administrator.

He serves as a mentor. I served the Asia LIFE University as its founding President for 16 years. I received inspiration in leading the ALU from Dr. Mathew's leadership and advice. I know several leaders of educational institutions in Korea who also received help from him. He likes to share his experiences as a pastor, administrator, and counselor with pastors in a very informal way. His stewardship in serving the Presidents, Provosts, his fellow professors and students at ORU which I observed for many years taught me a lot about being a servant leader. Sharing time with him was influential in developing my personal leadership style.

He is a leadership trainer through conferences and seminars. During Dr. Mathew's visits to Korea, he and I visited several major cities like Seoul, Pusan, Daejeon, Woolsan, Daegu, etc. to lead educational seminars and professional conferences for pastors. Pastors loved his teaching because he understood their thinking and difficulties. His teaching was easy to understand and practically applicable because it came from his life, studies, and ministry experiences.

Finally, Dr. Mathew is an excellent preacher, a Pentecostal preacher. When he meets people personally, he is very humble. However, once he stands on the pulpit, he delivers the message like a lion rebuking the darkness powerfully and at the same time showing the tender love of God. He preached several times at Yoido Full Gospel Church, the Healing Crusade Meetings at Dr. Cho's 6,000-seat Prayer Mountain, Korean Pentecostal Church Council's annual meetings, Bishop Yoo's Central Methodist Church which has more than 10,000 members, and several other venues. He prayed for salvation and healing of the people. Dr. Mathew always prepares himself for whatever the Lord asks him to do. It appears that since he prepares himself, the Lord keeps using him in different ways in various cultures and settings.

**Yeol Soo Eim, DMiss, Former President, Asia LIFE University, Daejeon, Korea; Former Director of the Korean DMin Program, Oral Roberts University**

I was privileged to work as Dr. Thomson Mathew's Administrative Assistant for the duration of his deanship of 16 years. His model of leadership was outstanding, and he took his responsibility as a leader seriously. He was sought after for his wisdom, and several other deans, his peers, also came to him for counsel. On occasion, his superiors did as well.

In his role as Dean, Dr. Mathew modeled how to work like a family with faculty, staff, and students alike. He truly cared about everyone and always worked to bring the best resolution to situations. As a strong leader, he never put himself first; he always worked for the best of others. He had an amazing ability to look at situations from the perspective of the weaker party. He had the admiration of everyone at the university who knew him, certainly of those who worked for him. He was a true leader.

On many occasions, I saw students walk into the Dean's Office determined to "do it their way" and then leave his office thanking him and with a completely different countenance and a smile on their faces. I noticed that there had been a transformation in their attitude while talking to him. He always extended grace but at the same time held the individuals accountable.

Dr. Mathew believed in teamwork and kept his Administrative Faculty updated regularly. His entire faculty admired and respected him highly. It was an honor to be a part of such a team led by an outstanding man of God.

**Judy Cope, Administrative Assistant to the Dean (2000-2016)**

I had the immense honor of receiving the very first Dean's Fellowship, a very generous scholarship package, offered in the Oral Roberts University (ORU) Graduate School of Theology and Ministry. In that role, I was incredibly privileged to serve as a research fellow for Dr. Thomson Mathew, the Dean at that time.

Just months prior to being granted the Fellowship, I had been working with a missions organization and had traveled to Barcelona, Spain, on a short-term exploratory trip. During that time, it became clear to me through several God-ordained circumstances that He wanted me to return to Tulsa and look into pursuing a master's degree in Biblical Literature. Previous to this, my thoughts concerning the future had not included seeking another degree. Yet, God made His will obvious when I applied for and received the sole Fellowship available for students attending the ORU Graduate School of Theology and Ministry.

The beginning of my first semester as a graduate student was very tumultuous. But I remember meeting with Dr. Mathew during that time. His reassurances regarding my selection as the Dean's Fellow gave continued confirmation as to where God had me. Moving into a new season with God is not always easy, but the difficulty can be a sign of future fruitfulness. And what a beautiful gift those three years proved to be! During that time, I worked closely with Judy Cope, Dr. Mathew's administrative assistant, on a variety of tasks. We became more than coworkers; we developed a close and supportive friendship that continues even today. In addition, what a joy it was to be involved with the many amazing professors, staff, and students of the Seminary and Undergraduate Department of Theology.

As I served Dr. Mathew through research, writing, and developing resources for his teaching, I benefited greatly under his leadership. His covering, spiritual and administrative, over the Seminary was significant and exceptional. Part of my job was working on resources for his teaching material. While I may have been helping him, it actually turned into a considerable blessing for me. Day after day, my spirit would be encouraged as I worked through his courses that were filled with the Word of God and truth. At other times, I was thankful for the excuse of helping him with his power-points in the classroom, which gave me the opportunity to attend the class and hear him teach. Among the students his lectures were a favorite, Spirit-filled and powerful, infused with stories, experiences, and wisdom. And whenever Dr. Mathew prayed, his prayers overflowed with praise and exultation of God. Dr. Mathew, along with his dear wife Molly, included me as family, which I recognized as a special privilege.

By the time I graduated from ORU, I not only gained a degree, but I was also given an extended family. Little did I know the incredible blessing God would bestow upon me when He called me to ORU and to this degree. This gift from Him came through a formal education, but also in the richness of relationships and the wisdom of those under whom God placed me and allowed me to serve.

**Heather Wright, Former Seminary Student and Theology Fellow**

In January 1981, I was completing five years as the pastor of the Sunriver Community Church in Sunriver, Oregon, a resort/residential community 17 miles south of Bend, Oregon, located in the Cascade Mountains at 4,200 feet above sea level. I was following the building of the City of Faith medical complex on the campus of Oral Roberts University through Oral Roberts' television programs. With my experience of having completed active duty in Vietnam and a tour of duty as a chaplain at the Navy Regional Medical Center in San Diego, I felt prompted to apply for a chaplaincy position at the still unopened City of Faith (COF). Following a hastily arranged interview on campus, I was hired to start work on July 1, 1981, three months before the opening of the Hospital.

I began service by working in the already open City of Faith Clinic and by visiting patients from the Clinic who were admitted in the St. John Hospital in Tulsa. It was during this period when I ran into Thomson Mathew in the lobby of the City of Faith. He had just completed his interview for a chaplaincy position. We visited for a few minutes, during which time I was prompted by the Holy Spirit to tell him he would be returning to serve at the City of Faith.

Shortly after the opening of the COF Hospital on November 1, 1981, I was appointed as the associate director of the Spiritual Care department. In this position, I had the opportunity to watch the young Thomson work with the interdisciplinary staff and serve the patients as a chaplain. He was clinically trained but was open to the Holy Spirit and worked with a sense of calling. During his time of service as a chaplain (called prayer partner at COF) and later as an administrator, I witnessed Thomson's work as a servant leader. While the City of Faith was still open, he was called to the ORU Seminary to serve as a professor and later, dean. Regardless of the positions he held, Thomson Mathew never forgot his roots or his calling. Although the City of Faith closed in 1989, we kept in touch with each other all these years, and served together on the board of a missions organization for more than three decades.

**David D. Dunning, DMin, City of Faith Chaplain and Associate Director**

I became a member of Gospel Tabernacle around 1970, a church at the corner of Orange and Edward Streets in New Haven, CT. The love of Christ was very much evident in this congregation. I became involved with the youth group and participated in several other activities designed to enhance fellowship among believers. Whenever a first-time visitor would attend, they were warmly greeted and welcomed.

On a particular Sunday, I was in the sanctuary when I noticed a young man I had not seen before, sitting nearby. His complexion was like mine, so I assumed he was of Hispanic descent, like me. I approached him and greeted him in Spanish. Much to my surprise, he didn't understand what I was saying! He told me his name—Thomson K. Mathew—and said that he was a preacher's kid from India and was attending Yale Divinity School. He had been looking for a Pentecostal church and his search led him to Gospel Tabernacle.

As time passed, he became a regular attendee, and we eventually became good friends. One day he gave me a tour of the Yale Divinity School. It was quite interesting. We began to have regular fellowship. One day, while on a visit to the Twin Towers at the World Trade Center in New York City, I had my first taste of Indian cuisine!

I recall visiting him later, while he was a chaplain at the Norwich State Hospital in Norwich, CT. Whenever I visited him there, we would always go to a well-known pizza place in downtown Norwich and indulge. My pizza-loving brother would later marry his sweetheart, Molly, and be blessed with two daughters, Amy and Jaime. He would also become the senior pastor of Gospel Tabernacle, a position he held for several years, during which, as a result of church growth and a building program, we were able to relocate to a new and much larger church building in North Haven, CT.

Through the years, we had so many wonderful times of fellowship and I learned how to be a better servant of the Lord, through his teachings and profound insights into God's Word. He was always a man of integrity, a doer of the Word, not just a hearer. He led by example. I will always cherish the countless memories of our times of fellowship in the Lord.

His time at Gospel Tabernacle ended when the Lord called him to join the staff at Oral Roberts University in Tulsa, OK. To this day, we still communicate with one another and will do so until Jesus comes!

**Sal Rivera, Former Tulsa Police Officer, and a Leader at Gospel Tabernacle**

# A Seminary Dean's
# EXPERIMENT with
# SERVANT LEADERSHIP

# A Seminary Dean's
# EXPERIMENT with
# SERVANT LEADERSHIP

Stories and Lessons from My Journey
Through Ivy League to Whole Person Education

**Thomson K. Mathew**

*A Seminary Dean's Experiment with Servant Leadership*

Copyright © 2021 by Thomson K. Mathew
*www.thomsonkmathew.com*

All rights reserved. No portion of this book may be reproduced, stored in a retrieval system, or transmitted in any form or by any means—electronic, mechanical, photocopy, recording, scanning, or other—except for brief quotations in critical reviews or articles, without the prior written permission of the author.

Published by:

GOODNEWS BOOKS
Kottayam, Kerala 686 004, India

Originally published independently in the United States.

Unless otherwise indicated, Scripture quotations are taken from the Holy Bible, New King James Version®. Copyright © 1982 by Thomas Nelson. Used by permission. All rights reserved.

Scripture quotations marked NIV are taken from the Holy Bible, New International Version®, NIV® Copyright ©1973, 1978, 1984, 2011 by Biblica, Inc.® Used by permission. All rights reserved worldwide.

Scripture quotations marked KJV are taken from the Holy Bible, King James Version (public domain).

ISBN: 978-1-7379780-0-8

Cover design: Creative Publishing Book Design
Cover photo: Image licensed by Shutterstock

To My Children and Grandchildren:
*Elizabeth and Fiju Koshy,*
*Jamie Ann Mathew,*
*Philip Thomson Koshy, and*
*Joseph Mathew Koshy*

# Contents

Introduction . . . . . . . . . . . . . . . . . . . . . . . xxi

Part I        My Story: A Seminary Dean From India
Chapter 1   Life in India . . . . . . . . . . . . . . . . . . . . . . . . . 3
Chapter 2   Yale and New Haven. . . . . . . . . . . . . . . . . 15
Chapter 3   Tulsa, City of Faith, and ORU . . . . . . . . . . 29
Chapter 4   A Seminary Serving the World . . . . . . . . . . 55

Part II       Stories
Chapter 5   Stories from India . . . . . . . . . . . . . . . . . . . 87
Chapter 6   Stories from Yale and New Haven . . . . . . . . 97
Chapter 7   Stories from City of Faith . . . . . . . . . . . . . 113
Chapter 8   Stories From ORU . . . . . . . . . . . . . . . . . . 135

Part III      Lessons
Chapter 9   Lessons on Ministry,
                 Leadership, and Life . . . . . . . . . . . . . . . . . 175

Appendix
Message One: I Change Not. . . . . . . . . . . . . . . . . . . . 213
Message Two: Moses, Joshua, and Who?. . . . . . . . . . . 219
Who Wants to Be a Messenger? . . . . . . . . . . . . . . . . . 225
Oral Tradition . . . . . . . . . . . . . . . . . . . . . . . . . . . . . . . 229

# Introduction

What you are reading is not a typical autobiography or memoir. Instead, this is primarily a collection of real-life stories, beginning with my own, but presenting some incredible people I met on my journey from a preacher's home in Kerala, India, through Yale University to the campus of Oral Roberts University (ORU) in Tulsa, Oklahoma, where I served thirty-seven years, including sixteen years as dean of the College of Theology and Ministry. The rest of this book contains reality tested and rarely available lessons on healthy ministry, servant leadership, and wholesome life distilled from these stories, and learned from thousands of students and many pastors and leaders around the world.

Built by a visionary and true son of Oklahoma—Oral Roberts, the renowned healing evangelist—Oral Roberts University is a global center for Christ-centered and Spirit-led whole person education. This unique institution that is represented by two iconic symbols—a prayer tower and the healing hands sculpture—has gained public interest, national attention, and international fame. It has been my privilege to be a servant leader at ORU as a chaplain, professor, and seminary dean for nearly four decades. A major part of this book is a personal record of history and stories about this unique place where Spirit-empowered leaders are developed. I write this as a servant of God and educator to inform, instruct, and inspire.

This book has three parts. As I am not well-known to many readers, Part One begins with a short version of my personal story. This is necessary to help the reader place the accompanying stories in their contexts. This part also contains the brief but rare story of the now-closed City of Faith Medical and Research Center where I served as a chaplain and administrator for eight years before joining the ORU Seminary faculty.

Part Two contains the many real-life stories as they are connected to three geographic locations. These are presented in four segments as stories from: 1) India where I grew up, 2) New Haven where I received theological education at Yale Divinity School and served as a local pastor, 3) City of Faith Medical and Research Center in Tulsa, and 4) Oral Roberts University.

Part Three presents the vital lessons I have learned during my pilgrimage regarding healthy ministry, successful leadership, and wholesome life. This section ends by emphasizing the importance of patience as God forms and shapes us as servant leaders.

The Appendix contains the summaries of two sermons I delivered to the ORU community at crucial moments. The speeches my daughters gave as ORU valedictorians (2000 and 2002) are also included in the Appendix to give the reader a taste of the spirit of whole person education.

All the stories in this book are true although some individuals' names are not used when it is appropriate. Only incidents I personally witnessed, experienced, or were publicly shared by the individuals involved are included. Due to the nature of the positions I held, there are some stories I cannot share.

This has been a difficult book to write because I have people in the USA and India, and in several places between these two nations that have impacted my life but there was no way to include everyone and still make the book readable for all. Excluding some has been painful.

I am grateful to my wife Molly who has encouraged me to document what you will find in this volume. She has been a part of and a witness of most of the stories you are about to encounter. My two daughters and two grandsons are a constant inspiration to me. I am now writing a fuller version of my story just for them.

I am grateful to April Kelly and Marlene Mankins for their editorial assistance. I wish to express my thanks to *Goodnews* Chief Editor C. V. Mathew for his support and assistance. I also want to thank my friends who contributed their voices in the opening pages of this book.

I thank God for the people who blessed me by being who they are, by participating in God's work with me wholeheartedly as I attempted to lead as a servant, and by investing in my life in so many ways. I remain grateful to each one.

I dedicate this book as an offering to God and present it to my readers with the sincere prayer that they would find a measure of encouragement, inspiration, and instruction in these pages.

Thomson K. Mathew
*www.thomsonkmathew.com*

*Part I*

# My Story: A Seminary Dean From India

*Chapter 1*

# Life In India

## Born in God's Own Country

I was born in a house on the outskirts of a small town called Erumely in the eastern part of Kerala state, the evergreen southwestern state of India. Known for the highest literacy rate in the nation and considered the cradle of Christianity in India due to the coming of Saint Thomas in AD 52, Kerala is now called "God's own country" and "the Kashmir of the South." The small village where I was born was at the edge of a lush forest area. When I was born, my mother, Aleyamma, was beginning her career as an elementary school teacher and my father, K. T. Mathew, was being mentored to be a pastor by two of his uncles who were well-known Pentecostal preachers.

My parents were newcomers in my place of birth, from a town called Niranam which was famous for the church at the heart of it that was founded by Saint Thomas in AD 54.

Niranam had one of the seven churches believed to have been founded by Saint Thomas with many famous legends among both the Hindus and Christians concerning the miracles Thomas performed 2,000 years ago that led to the establishment of the church. The original church building was renovated several times and during the third major renovation in AD 1259, a large all-granite cross was installed near the main entrance to the church. My father's parents were proud members of this historic church. They lived about half a mile south of the church on a country lane that passed through paddy fields and coconut groves. My father was the oldest of their five children in a family that had some cultural symbols of previous wealth, but lived modestly in this area that cultivated sugarcane and rice. When I grew up, as the oldest of six children—two boys and four girls—both my father and grandfather were Pentecostal ministers serving in different parts of Kerala.

Extended morning and evening prayers involving the entire household was the norm in my family. Normally these prayers lasted thirty minutes to an hour each time. At least two chapters from the Bible were read and every family member prayed beginning with the youngest child. It was not uncommon to have some of us fully asleep when the prayer time was over. The prayer time ended with the recitation of the Lord's prayer. My sister Leela fell asleep more often than the others. Sometimes I found her sound asleep on her knees after everybody had been gone after prayer. I remember teasing her by whispering the beginning of the Lord's prayer in her ear, which she recited frantically without opening her eyes. I enjoyed watching her open her eyes after hearing no one else praying along and realize what happened.

Although these prayer times were long sessions, they planted biblical truths deeply in all our hearts. No wonder all my siblings—Annie, Leela, John, Jaya, and Valsa—are involved in ministry today. I remember attending many church services and cottage meetings in the evenings during my childhood where I fell asleep and had to be awakened before going home. However, like all preacher's kids, I heard almost all my father's sermons during those days, and they had an impact on my life.

When I was ten years old, I accepted Christ as my savior and experienced the baptism of the Holy Spirit. I was not baptized in water for four years because my father did not believe that I had a full understanding of baptism. I was a high school student at St. Mary's High School at Niranam, a school belonging to the Orthodox church, when I was baptized by my father in a creek. We had relocated from Erumely to Niranam by then.

## At Mar Thoma College

I graduated from high school in 1966, with a "first class" designation. It was not clear what I would do after high school. Going to Bible college or full-time ministry preparation was not on the agenda. The only discussion we had was that I could follow the footsteps of two cousins who had joined the Indian Air Force. Unfortunately, when I graduated from high school, I was too young and too small to be recruited. Thinking that I must keep myself occupied as a student until I got old enough and big enough to possibly join the Indian Air Force, my parents decided to send me to Mar Thoma College in Thiruvalla, another Christian institution managed by the Mar Thoma Church and affiliated with Kerala University. My mother applied for a government scholarship that was available to teachers' children. I qualified and received it and that made the college plan easier. I enrolled in a pre-degree (PDC) program with the major study area called "first group" which allowed students to study mathematics, physics, and chemistry, along with English and Hindi. There was a choice of language between Hindi and Malayalam. I chose Hindi thinking that it would help my life in North India where I expected to go in the future for better employment as several other relatives had.

## To Bishop Moore College

I completed the pre-degree (PDC) program successfully at Mar Thoma College in 1968. By then, the idea of joining the Air Force had dissipated and a career in teaching or science became the focus because everyone who studied the first group in those days dreamed about getting a job in the newly acclaimed atomic energy commission of India, near Bombay. My father's brother, Thomas Nainan, was working in a British chemical company in Bombay then which gave fuel to this wish. My family decided to send me to undergraduate studies in Physics at Bishop Moore College (BMC)—a college belonging to the Church of South India (CSI) and currently listed among the top 100 colleges in India—in Mavelikara, the town where my father was beginning a new pastorate.

## A Seminary Dean's Experiment with Servant Leadership

A Church of South India clergyman, Rev. K. C. Mathew, was the college principal. The students in the Physics class were some of the brightest on campus. We were all afraid of the principal who held graduate degrees in Physics and Religious Education. Whenever he went by our classroom during his routine "veranda walks," we all sat still, paying close attention to the lecturer in the class. The institution, affiliated with Kerala University, had a brand-new beautiful campus with modern labs, a library, and other facilities, including a chapel. Chapel services were held regularly. The principal had a special interest in our class because of his background in Physics.

I enjoyed my studies and made the most wonderful friends at Bishop Moore College. Amazingly, after half a century, some of us have reconnected through the internet and are now keeping our college friendships alive. Friends such as Hariprasad S. (Hari), an Indian Army colonel living in Bangalore; Remadevi D. (Rema), a female principal of a boy's high school in Kerala; Muralidharan A., a bank officer; Gopakumar P., an officer in the Customs and Central Excise department; and two immigrants: Babu P. Alex in Houston and Saram Philip in New York City, all now retired. We have enjoyed two reunions with the classmates in India. The years I spent at Bishop Moore College were life transforming in terms of academic development and personal formation. My life goals changed while I was a student there.

### Story Writing Ends

The above-mentioned Hari, Babu, and I were like triplets on campus. So much so that we received the nickname "three flowers," partially because those words were in the lyrics of an immensely popular contemporary movie song. We were involved in the publishing of the college magazine through a student representative position Hari held. We wanted to contribute to the magazine and co-authored a short story. Of course, the title of our story was "Three Flowers." We thought it was a great love story, but I cannot remember any of the characters or plot now. I was so proud to see the love story in print with our names clearly printed in the byline. I left a copy of the magazine, titled *Sruthi* (Harmony) on my study table at home. When I noticed it a few days later, I was surprised to see a word written on its cover in my father's handwriting. The word was "Apasruthi" (Disharmony). I knew my secular literary future was coming to an end.

My first article in a Christian magazine named *Christ's Soldiers* came out when I was in my early teens. I received a lot of commendations from my parents and grandparents then. I have no doubt why my writing still involves only non-fiction Christian content. Parental approval and guidance are amazingly influential!

## A Sense of Calling

I began to sense a call to ministry during my years at Bishop Moore College. Several things influenced me in this regard. First was my participation in ministry activities with my father and active involvement in youth ministry in my home church and the area churches of our denomination (India Pentecostal Church—IPC). The youth wing of IPC,

## A Seminary Dean's Experiment with Servant Leadership

called the Pentecostal Young People's Association (PYPA), gave me several opportunities to serve in leadership positions. The chapel services at BMC were an inspiration to me as they planted thoughts of entering ministry in the future. Additionally, BMC had an annual scripture knowledge competition with a highly regarded prize. Even though I was a Physics major, and the college did not have a Theology or Bible department, two out of my three years there, I won the first place in this competition and received volumes of Christian books as awards, including a Bible which my father bound in leather and preserved after I left home. I now have that Bible.

These prizes reflected the impact of two well-known evangelistic ministries on my life—India Every Home Crusade and All India Prayer Fellowship. I had successfully completed Bible correspondence courses offered by both these organizations. Additionally, on behalf of the India Every Home Crusade, a high school friend, Babu Abraham, and I got involved in door-to-door gospel tract distribution. All these experiences were revealing my aptitude for Christian ministry in a cumulative way. A Billy Graham crusade held near our house where Graham's associate, Abdul Haq, preached added to my sense of calling. I remember imitating Rev. Haq's preaching in my physics classroom during breaks! As a result of listening to him, preaching the gospel became a matter of importance in my life.

My final year in college, 1971, was the silver jubilee year of the Pentecostal Young People's Association (PYPA). The annual state-wide PYPA conference (called camp) that year was held at Ernakulam, a city near Cochin. I was able to attend this camp where a state-wide elocution competition was held. It involved signing up to do a public speech which was graded by a panel of judges. The topic was given to each participant only five minutes prior to giving the speech. As one participant began the speech, the next one got the topic in a closed room away from the podium where the contestant could not hear the other speaker. Those were the most punishing minutes as one was forced to develop the given topic and organize it mentally at such a high speed. It was a nightmare to someone like me who had both stage fright and test anxiety.

I remember receiving the topic, something like "the Bible and Science" or "Faith and Science," and being extremely nervous as I tried to develop and organize my thoughts on the subject. I had some experience in speech competitions at the local and district levels in PYPA, but never at the state level. I got through my speech and felt that it went well but was surprised when I was announced as the first prize winner. I will never forget the service in which Pastor K. E. Abraham, the esteemed founding leader of IPC, presented me with an award certificate. I was full of joy as I received congratulations from a host of people, many of whom came from reputable colleges. I still have that certificate in my possession because of the special meaning it has had in my life.

Some unusual incidents took place during this period. One of them involved a group of young people who visited me one day when I was home alone. I heard a knock on the door and opened it to find a group of young people standing there. It was obvious that they were going from house to house, distributing gospel tracts. As soon as I opened the door, the person who looked like the leader of the group said, "This is the person I saw." As I gave him a puzzled look, he asked my permission to come in. I let the group come into the house, seated them, and offered them some water to drink. As they settled down, the leader said something like this: "We have been going from house to house distributing gospel tracts and sharing our faith with those who would listen. We took a break to enjoy some coffee and snacks. As we prayed over the food, your face came to my mind, and I got the impression that I would meet you today and should give you a message."

This is the summary of the message he gave me: "God is calling you for his work. He will send you to a faraway country to be trained and will use you in ways beyond what you can imagine now." I listened to his words in disbelief as I just sat there. I was already wondering why they came with tracts to our residence, a parsonage attached to a worship hall which had a large sign clearly visible from the street, saying "India Pentecostal Church, Salem Hall." I did not know what to do with the information but was impacted by the whole incident. The group prayed for me and left soon, and I have never met any of them since that day. I could not wait for my parents to come home so I could tell them what happened. When I told my parents about the incident, they reminded me of a visiting evangelist who had prophesied to me some years earlier, basically saying similar things.

While I was a student at Bishop Moore College, Rev. G. Samuel[1], one of the uncles who had mentored my father, made several preaching tours in America. Unbeknown to me, he was trying to help me to get an opportunity to study in America. Based on his advice, I began correspondence with Yale Divinity School and submitted a formal application.

A few months after I graduated from Bishop Moore College with a BS in physics, I received formal admission to Yale Divinity School with a scholarship. I was supposed to begin my studies in fall 1971, but I did not receive the acceptance letter in time to begin studies then. Yale understood my predicament and extended my enrollment to fall 1972. I involved myself in working with my father in our church and in the local and district levels of PYPA.

My family went through a period of excitement and sadness, hope and despair, and a lot of pride as I prepared to leave for higher studies. A few days before my leaving, Pastor K. E. Abraham came to our church to preach. My grandfather also arrived from Niranam to attend that service. At the end

---

1 My paternal grandmother's grandfather Rev. Ninan Abraham (1847-1918) was a priest who was among the clergy who fought to reform the Orthodox (Jacobite) Church and at the end became a priest in the newly founded Mar Thoma Church. In the next generation, his younger son Mathews who was a Mar Thoma priest was involved in the efforts to reform the Mar Thoma Church and became a leader among the founding clergy of the St. Thomas Evangelical Church of India. In the following generation, my grandmother's sister Rachelamma led the way to Pentecostalism and her brother Rev. T. N. Abraham became the general secretary of the India Pentecostal Church. He and Rachelamma's husband Rev. G. Samuel mentored my father. See Joyan Kumarakom, *Pastor T. N. Abraham: A Surrendered Servant of God – A Biography* (Kottayam, Kerala: Good News Publications, 1999).

of the service, before the benediction, Rev. Abraham asked me to come forward and kneel. I obeyed. He asked my father to lay his hands on me. Then he asked my grandfather to lay his hands over my father's hands. He then laid his hands over their hands and prayed for me to set me apart to study the word of God and become a minister of the gospel. That moment, which happened several years before I was formally ordained, was frozen in my soul so strongly that throughout my life, especially at crucial times, I revisited that experience and gained strength from it. Whenever I face a major challenge in ministry, I still recall that moment from IPC Salem Hall, Mavelikara, which reminds me that I did not put myself in the challenging spot, but was commissioned as a servant of God to follow a legacy of generational service to God, and that thought calms me down.

*Chapter 2*

# Yale And New Haven

## At Yale Divinity School (YDS)

Leaving home for the first time, especially to a far-away land with only the guarantee of a letter and just eight dollars in cash—the maximum amount of money the government of India allowed citizens to take out of India in those days—was not easy, but I did not know enough about the world to be afraid of making such a trip. I landed in New York and stayed two days with my father's cousin, John Varghese, who had come to America before me. Accompanied by him, his wife, another relative, George Abraham, who later became a career officer at the United Nations, and his roommate, I arrived on Yale campus in New Haven two days before fall semester commenced in 1972. I was given a private room in the Bushnell dormitory, and I went through the registration process and orientation sessions. Disoriented to time and place, I began to attend classes.

On my first Sunday in New Haven, I did not know any church in town and did not know where to go to worship. Yale Divinity School had chapel services during weekdays but due to student pastorates in local churches, there were no chapel services held on Sundays. For the same reason, the cafeteria—called the Refectory—was also closed on Sundays. It was a cold Sunday and I realized that my suit jacket was not going to be sufficient to keep me warm. People on campus seemed to be okay, but having just come from tropical Kerala, that fall day felt very cold to me, but I did not want to miss worship. I decided to walk the streets to look for a church, preferably a Pentecostal church. I started on Prospect Street, turned left on Edward Street, and crossed Whitney Avenue and found a church building with the name Gospel Tabernacle, a beautiful old brick building with huge stained-glass windows.

I entered the building through the side door on Edward Street, which served as the major entrance, although there was a grander door on Orange Street. As I walked into the sanctuary, the congregation was singing, "He brought me to his banqueting table and his banner over me is love." I felt comfortable as it looked like a Pentecostal worship. Someone seated me in a curved pew, and I had my first worship service in the United States in New Haven, Connecticut, in an almost exclusively white church. At that time, I had no idea and there was no way to imagine that I would become the pastor of this congregation in less than five years. This building, with several huge custom-made stained-glass windows documenting the history of the original Methodist congregation, was a New Haven landmark. At that time, I did not know that it was about to become a landmark in my life as the place where I would get married, and where my firstborn daughter would be dedicated.

## The Kaisers

Several people spoke to me after the service, including a friendly young man named Sal Rivera who spoke to me first in Spanish, assuming that I was a person of Hispanic descent, but soon changed to English. He would become a life-long friend. Prominent among the people I met that day were Edith and Walter Kaiser, a couple who showed a special interest in my background and situation. When they discovered that I had walked to church, they offered to give me a ride back to the campus. As I walked out of the church with the Kaisers, a senior citizen who introduced herself as Mrs. Edna Livingstone shook my hand. She placed two one-dollar bills in my hand. I was surprised but accepted the gift and thanked her. I consider her gift to be the largest gift I have ever received as it told me clearly that the Lord would meet my needs in his own way in the new land.

The Kaisers asked me more questions about my life in the car as we drove to 409 Prospect Street, where I lived. As I opened the car door to leave, they told me that they had picked up other Yale students on Sundays in the past and would be glad to pick me up at the main gate next week if I wanted to return to that church. They gave me their phone number. As I watched them drive away, I did not realize that I had just begun a lifelong relationship with "mom" and "dad" Kaiser who would become "grandpa" and "grandma" to my daughters.

I heard a knock on my door a few days after my visit to Gospel Tabernacle at about 8 PM. I opened the door and was surprised to find Mr. and Mrs. Kaiser standing there. Mr. Kaiser was carrying a big package. They said it took them a long time to find my room as they did not know my dorm name or my room number. The divinity school quadrangle was designed in a unique way, with several dorms on both sides of the main entrance on Prospect Street as one moved up to the Marquand chapel at the center of the campus. Apartments for married students were behind the main area which housed the classrooms, chapel, and the library. The Kaisers had gone through several dorms already, checking with students to locate me. Mr. Kaiser gave me the package and asked me to open it. I was almost in tears when I saw a very warm winter coat with an attached hood! I was told that Mrs. Kaiser—an immigrant from Lithuania via Germany during World War II—had a dream in which she felt impressed to buy me a coat. I was most grateful. I kept that coat as a memorial for at least two decades.

In a few days they brought me a small metal desk that could serve as an end table that they had bought at a garage sale and repainted. I have refused to give up that desk and still have it with the original paint, as another reminder of God's faithfulness.

Forty-eight years after our first meeting, Walter Kaiser recently visited us in Florida. In his late eighties now, he lives with his daughter in Missouri. Mrs. Edith Kaiser passed away a few years ago. It was our privilege to attend her funeral in Springfield, Missouri, and tell the story of our relationship.

We continue to stay in touch with a couple of generations of Kaisers.

## Memories of YDS

I was one of the first Pentecostals to attend YDS but felt completely accepted by the campus community. The courses were challenging, and the amount of required reading was high. The professors expected excellence but were very pastoral in their approach to students, especially to international students who needed time to adjust to the place and in my case, to the new field of study. A non-traditional three-part grading system was in effect—Pass, High Pass, and Honors.

Abraham Malherbe's New Testament courses still linger in my soul. His lectures in the last sessions of the semester moved the class as scholarship and good news embraced each other tightly in them. At that time, I did not realize the lasting impact Mr. Rowan Greer's Luke lectures and David Kelsey's theology classes would have on my life and ministry, as I was just trying to grasp the material and pass the courses. How blessed I was to live on campus when Henri Nouwen was the big attraction! *The Wounded Healer* was the talk of the town. The long line of my classmates at his door was an ever-present sight. He dedicated his book, *The Living Reminder*, to YDS graduates in 1977, the year I received the STM degree. Years later, I made his writings required reading for the pastoral care and field education courses at ORU. My field education supervisors at the Masonic Home in Wallingford—Rev. Tom Schulz—and The Community Mental Health Center in

New Haven—Robert Anderson—helped me to put feet to my classroom learning. Professor Charles Miller quietly kept persuading students to keep Christian mission before us in everything we did.

Roland Bainton, the author of *Here I Stand*, was professor emeritus but a constant presence on campus in those days. He enjoyed joining students in the refectory for meals and conversations. It was his hobby to pencil-sketch the profiles of selected students during the meals and present them to the students. I still have my profile he sketched. His annual presentation of the Christmas story—devotional, humorous, and critical at the same time—was a campus ritual.

Dean Collin Williams, Harry Baker, Raymond Wood, and Joan Forsberg ran a smooth administration at YDS. Robert Nadonley managed the refectory. I was a student worker in his office.

Music from *Jesus Christ Superstar* blared out of the dorms. Watergate divided the campus. Some students streaked across the campus. Coed dormitory bathrooms freaked out some of us. Loud weekend parties sent me away to the Kaisers' house.

With the color-coded meal card, Yale students could eat at any of the dining halls on campus. I used to join some friends for meals in the law school dining hall but do not recall running into two students who graduated in 1973—one Bill Clinton and one Hillary Rodham Clinton!

I lived on campus during my Master of Divinity (MDiv) studies and lived off campus during the two years of studies for the Master of Sacred Theology (STM) in Pastoral Theology, which included a year of Clinical Pastoral

Education (CPE) in Norwich, CT. I participated in two Yale graduation ceremonies, in 1975 (MDiv) and 1977 (STM). President Gerald Ford gave the commencement address in 1977. Looking back at the campus on that day as I left with Molly and the Kaisers, I noticed the grandeur of the Sterling Memorial Library, the centerpiece of the library system at Yale. Recalling the huge size of the library collection and the tiny number of books I had read in my five years of study, I left Yale with a humbling realization of my lack of knowledge. That feeling never left me, and it turned me into a lifelong learner and an advocate for continuing professional education of ministers.

## Clinical Pastoral Education (CPE)

As I approached MDiv graduation in 1975, I considered leaving Yale for another school to pursue the Master of Sacred Theology (STM) degree. I applied to Yale, Princeton, and Duke University Divinity School. I wanted to do the STM or ThM in pastoral theology with the possibility of including Clinical Pastoral Education (CPE) as part of the requirements of that degree. Princeton did not accept me but kept corresponding, but I was accepted to the ThM program at Duke University Divinity School, and to the STM at Yale. When I considered the challenges and expenses of moving to another campus and of leaving the Kaisers behind, I decided to stay in New Haven and complete the degree at YDS and applied to be accepted into the CPE program at Norwich Hospital in Norwich, Connecticut. I was encouraged to enroll in CPE by Justice Akrofi, a classmate who had completed CPE at

Norwich and who, years later, became the archbishop of the Anglican Church of West Africa.

I graduated from YDS with an MDiv in May 1975, and was accepted into the CPE residency program at Norwich Hospital. Clinical Pastoral Education at Norwich was to be the first year of my post-MDiv STM studies in pastoral theology. This training helped me significantly, not only by giving me better pastoral care and counseling skills, but also by increasing my self-understanding and ministerial identity. Rev. Robert Erickson was my CPE supervisor. He was a disciple of Clarence Bruninga who was trained by Anton Boisen who is considered the father of CPE. When he demanded pastoral excellence and confronted me on many occasions, I did not realize what a lasting positive impact Erickson would have on my life. During the first quarter of CPE, Erickson's assistant, Rick Osmer, who later became a well-known practical theologian, also challenged my group of CPE residents. Osmer now serves at Princeton where my MDiv classmate Deborah van Deusen Hunsinger serves as an expert in pastoral care and counseling.

During my year at Norwich, a non-Pentecostal church—Poquannock Bridge Baptist Church in Groton, CT—hired me as a pastor's assistant and Christian educator. I spent weekends involved in adult education and periodic preaching at the church and made many local friends. While filling in on a communion Sunday for the vacationing pastor, Rev. Richard Strong, I ran into some surprise and embarrassment as a newly elected deacon had kept the trays of communion cups filled with authentic Welch's grape juice in the freezer overnight!

## Ordination and Surprise Pastorate

While working at Norwich Hospital, I was also pursuing ordination with the Southern New England District of the Assemblies of God (AG). Thankfully, this District granted me a license to preach first and ordained me in 1976 in Stamford, CT. As I was finishing CPE at Norwich, Rev. Leroy Whiteman who pastored Gospel Tabernacle during my student days at YDS resigned and I was asked to be a pulpit supply there while the church was on a pastoral search. The church promised me residence at its parsonage in Hamden, Connecticut—a five-bedroom unfurnished house on a hill on Troiano Street—and $75 a week pay. I accepted the offer and moved to the parsonage in June 1976, with plans to move my residence to Yale campus in the fall.

On July 20, 1976, at about 8:30 PM, I received a call at the parsonage from the deacon board of Gospel Tabernacle. They shared with me that at the business meeting held that night to consider a pastoral candidate, the church members voted against the candidate and instead elected me as their pastor. I had never even applied for the position and had not been consulted. I was flattered but was really in shock because such an offer was not a simple matter in my case, because I was not a legal permanent resident of this country at that time and was not eligible to accept a full-time job. I had to inform the church that I was on a student visa and not eligible to accept the position unless they were willing to sponsor me to become an immigrant. An immigrant visa was not a guaranteed document in my case because the immigration rules in those days required the applicant to have three years of

*23*

fulltime ministry experience to qualify for a religious worker's visa. Additionally, I was not willing to give up my theological education. So, I asked the church if they were willing to let me continue my studies at Yale to complete the STM degree. The church agreed to my requests, and I was installed as pastor.

Being a full-time student and a full-time pastor was exciting, challenging, and at times discouraging. For example, during my first week as senior pastor, a man who was a prominent member of the church passed away and I had to minister to the family and conduct the funeral services. There was one problem: I had not even seen an American funeral service at that point. Fortunately, we had a retired pastor in the congregation, Rev. Theodore Johanson, Sr., who gave me much instruction. I also called a couple of neighboring pastors and sought their advice and help. The elder son of the deceased was a prominent pastor in Chicago and his brother, Alan Ciociola, was the pianist for the world-renowned *Revival Time Choir* of the Assemblies of God, whom we hired later as our minister of music. By the grace of God, I was able to conduct the funeral and continue as pastor, thanks be to God and to the longsuffering and patience of the church members who allowed me to learn to become a pastor on the job.

The church began to grow. I can only attribute the growth to the grace of God because I had no experience in pastoring or church growth. I had seen my father and grandfather pastor in India and tried to imitate their ministry in a contextualized way. Also, I was more a chaplain than a pastor at that time by training. In my enthusiasm for pastoral counseling, I put ads in the phonebook saying that we offered free counseling. That

## A Seminary Dean's Experiment with Servant Leadership

brought interesting new church members! I also placed ads in the daily New Haven Register (one titled "Wanted: Sinners") and in Yale Daily News ("Man Shall Not Live by Scholarship Alone!"). In the pre-multimedia generation, these unusual ads did get noticed and we had regular visitors from the community and Yale campus. Many joined our church. As the church grew, our facilities became inadequate, but upgrading the old building with high ceiling and leaky beautiful windows and adding a parking lot became impossible at the corner of Orange and Edward.

It so happened that a lady in North Haven owned 10.3 acres of land and wanted to sell it at a reasonable price to the local church where she was a member. As we learned that her church declined her offer, we reached out to her. We were able to purchase the 10.3 acres off interstate highway I-91 on Montowese Avenue just few blocks from the highway for only $75,000. People had mixed feelings about moving out of New Haven as there were strong emotions attached to the old building and the history of the church. But a vote was taken, and a decision was made to move out. A few families were not able to make that move and decided to attend other churches in the area.

After we bought the land in North Haven to build the new church, someone donated a cornerstone with scripture verses, my name, and the year 1978 inscribed on it. I was not even 27 years old yet, and was the senior pastor involved in building a house of worship with a sanctuary, conference room, classrooms, and offices, together about 20,000 square feet of space on 10.3 acres of prime land. It seemed like things had a life of their own and I was just along for the ride. I did not have to push to make anything happen. Although there was considerable stress involved, it seemed like doors simply opened and we were just walking through them with a group of excited disciples of Jesus. I gratefully remember four associate pastors who shared this journey with us—Don Rudolph, Alan Ciociola, Dan Jones, and Greg Boyd who later became a globally recognized theologian—and an excellent office manager, Ruth Vergason.

## Marriage and Family

Meanwhile, on October 30, 1976, I married Molly, the daughter of a pastor who served in the same IPC district with my father back in Kerala and the granddaughter of a widely recognized Pentecostal pioneer in Kerala, Rev. K. C. John. She was the oldest of three, with a brother Stephen and a sister Molsy, who was brought to this country as a professional nurse by her father's friend, Rev. T. O. Oommen, who was a Methodist pastor in Southwick, Mass. As mentioned earlier, I had expected to complete the pulpit supply ministry at Gospel Tabernacle by the end of August 1976, move out of the parsonage, and begin studies full-time on campus starting September. However, within weeks after the decision to appoint me, I was installed as pastor of the church by the district superintendent Ryder Jacobson.

Jacobson was a wonderful pastor to me and a good mentor, but he kept calling me frequently to ask when I was going to get married. He said each time that I was too young, and there were too many young women in the church near a university, and that the wisest thing for me was to get married as soon as possible. I kept telling him that I did not have a girlfriend, but he was relentless. I felt really depressed after some of his calls, especially as the church began to see some growth in a short period of time. I thought the superintendent would be happy to hear about the church growing noticeably in such a short time, but it only increased his worry about my potential moral failure and the frequency of his calls, so I was glad when Rev. T. O. Oommen called me and introduced me to Molly.

Once a decision was made regarding our marriage, with our parents' reluctant permission, Molly stayed with the Kaisers for a short period of time and got oriented to life in the community. The wedding ceremony took place at the church and Rev. Jacobson officiated. Because of finances and visa problems, our families could not attend our wedding. John Varghese from New York was the best man. His wife was the maid of honor. Church members played all other parts in the ceremony. The Kaisers stood in my parents' place and the Oommens acted as Molly's parents, while the church took care of all the details of the simple reception that followed. Walter Kaiser's father, Leo, a professional baker, donated the wedding cake!

God blessed us with two daughters—Elizabeth Susan whom we call "Amy" and Jamie Ann. Both were dedicated by Rev. Hugh Corey, the superintendent who followed Rev. Jacobson, Amy in the old Gospel Tabernacle and Jamie in the new building in North Haven. Born in New England and raised in Oklahoma, Amy graduated from Oral Roberts University as valedictorian (class speaker) and earned her PhD in Counseling Psychology from Texas Woman's University in Denton, Texas. She is a licensed psychologist and is married to Dr. Fiju Koshy, a physician who completed his residency at the In His Image Family Practice Residency Program in Tulsa led by Dr. John Crouch, a former Oral Roberts University (ORU) Medical School professor. They made us proud grandparents of two boys—Philip Thomson Koshy and Joseph Mathew Koshy. Following her sister, Jamie graduated as valedictorian from Oral Roberts University and went on to earn a JD degree from the University of Oklahoma College of Law and an MBA from Southern Nazarene University. She is licensed in three states, and practices law as a litigator.

*Chapter 3*

# Tulsa, City of Faith, and ORU

## To Oklahoma, the Indian Country

As the new church building in North Haven began to get filled up with newly added members from North Haven, I began to feel that my ministry there was coming to an end. I had been feeling for a while that I would eventually be involved in training people for ministry. My idea at that time of how that would look was becoming a CPE supervisor in a hospital or a field education director in a seminary. Both required further training or a doctorate. The Doctor of Ministry (DMin) was becoming established as a terminal degree at that time. I inquired about enrolling at different seminaries and informed the church board of my desire. But the board felt that I was already over-qualified and needed no further theological education. I began to think about the possibility of leaving the pastorate for a doctoral program with possible employment as a chaplain or pursuing a paid position as a CPE supervisor-in-training.

Molly and I had visited the ORU campus as tourists with some people from Mississippi we accidentally met at a conference in Oklahoma City in 1977. I was impressed with the famous prayer tower at the center of the campus and the history of the university that was presented in a multimedia presentation at the visitors' center. Later, I became aware of Oral Roberts' plan to build the City of Faith Medical and Research Center to "merge medicine and prayer." I also knew that ORU Seminary was launching the DMin program. I kept up with the progress there through television programs and Roberts' magazine, *Abundant Life*. I began correspondence with the Seminary and the Oral Roberts Ministries regarding the possibility of working as a chaplain in the new hospital and enrolling in the DMin program at ORU.

Having received nothing but a cold acknowledgement letter, I accepted a staff chaplain position at Norwich Hospital offered by Bob Erickson. Within few weeks, I was surprised to receive a call from City of Faith Hospital, asking me to come to Tulsa for an interview for a chaplain position. I flew to Tulsa and was met by Dr. Jimmy Buskirk, former professor at Candler School of Theology at Emory University and dean of the ORU Seminary, and Dr. Duie Jernigan, a retired (colonel) army chaplain who had just been appointed to head up the Spiritual Care Division at the City of Faith. I met Oral Roberts during that visit; he told me about his crusade in Trivandrum, capital of Kerala, and the invitation he received from the Travancore maharaja to pray for his wife (the queen) who was ill. He told me about going to the palace and praying for the Hindu queen and seeing her recover.

I did not know if I had the job at the end of the visit, but as I was being driven back to the airport by Dr. and Mrs. Jernigan, Mrs. Norma Jernigan laughingly told me to go and pack to come back. The colonel kept silent. I received a formal offer to be the first staff chaplain at the hospital a few days later. A clinic was previously open at the City of Faith, and there were chaplains working there already, including Rev. David Dunning, the designated associate director of chaplaincy in the soon-to-be opening hospital. Rev. Erickson released me to go to Tulsa as he recognized City of Faith as a better place for my future.

## "Merging Medicine and Prayer" at City of Faith

The City of Faith was a place of excitement. Professionals from all over the country came to be a part of the story of attempting to merge scientific medicine with spiritual care in a place affiliated with an international healing ministry, an accredited medical school that had a respected faculty, the latest technology, and the most enviable new facilities (the complex had 2 million square feet of floor space and was the tallest building in the state at that time.) The fact that a television healing evangelist was pioneering this effort caught the attention of the nation and the field of medicine.

Oral Roberts was a household name at that time and his partners sent sacrificial gifts to make sure the construction of the facility was without debt. The complex contained three towers, one 20-story research center, a 60-story clinic, and a third which was designated as the hospital with 30 stories. The design of the building was futuristic and avoided much of the inconveniences of traditional hospitals. For example, traditional hospitals have long hallways where patients and visitors can get lost easily. The rooms in the City of Faith towers were designed as suites called alcoves with computers in each alcove, all built around circular hallways. [Computers were not in general use in those days and the internet was not even a public concept.] It was practically impossible to get lost on any floor as the design made sure that you would come back to the same place by walking forward, making sure you were able to reach an elevator to leave the floor if needed, regardless of the direction in which you walked.

Oral Roberts University had a reputable faculty in its medical school and many new doctors were hired to staff the clinic attached to the hospital and to do follow-up work there. ORU had a school of nursing that was producing outstanding nurses, but in addition to ORU graduates, nurses were hired from across the country. Similarly other medical professionals and staff were added to the team. All were confessing Christians, and most were members of the Pentecostal/charismatic movement. It was a historic time in that the charismatic movement at that point was not generally open to medical care as the Pentecostals used to be before this time. Oral Roberts was sharing a revolutionary idea that God used natural and supernatural means to heal. Most of the people saw Oral Roberts on television and thought of him only as a person who believed in healing through prayer. But even earlier than this time Oral Roberts had documented his support of merging the natural and the supernatural.

A 60-foot-tall healing-hands sculpture stood in front of the City of Faith, and it was installed at the source of a well-designed "healing stream" with fountains at both ends. Roberts explained that one hand represented the hand of Paul who was a praying minister, and the other hand represented the hand of Luke, the evangelist who was a physician by profession. In the beginning of the opening of the hospital, finances were not a concern as excited Christians and partners of Oral Roberts' Ministry sent money to support this important effort. A significant portion of Oral Roberts' supporters were senior citizens and people of modest means. Many of them were sending $77 per square foot to build the City of Faith, most of them sponsoring only one square foot.

There was a great controversy surrounding the building and opening of the City of Faith. Competing hospitals in Tulsa launched active campaigns against the building and opening of the City of Faith Hospital. The claim was that a small town like Tulsa did not need the additional hospital beds. The local media were not supportive of the new effort. Oral Roberts was able to mobilize his supporters to let state and national leaders know that his partners supported the project and expected to utilize the hospital in the future, thereby demonstrating that these additional hospital beds would not be aimed at just Tulsa residents. Ultimately, the City of Faith received official permission to open with less than 300 beds with the plans to expand the number of beds to 777, and the facility was formally inaugurated on November 1, 1981.

Although doctors and other medical professionals had come to the City of Faith to practice medicine in a new way by attempting to merge medicine and prayer, no one had come with any experience doing it. The idea was to create healing teams consisting of doctors, nurses, and ministers who were called staff prayer partners rather than chaplains, and other professionals to deal with each patient in a multidisciplinary approach with prayer being equally valued as any other medical procedure. Everyone was encouraged to engage in prayer. Doctors and nurses and other professionals prayed, and each patient had an assigned "staff prayer partner" (chaplain) to help them with their spiritual care and to assist them in prayer. Incoming patients received prayer by the screening doctors and nurses and those admitted received prayer from the prayer partners and medical staff on the hospital floors. Patients received prayer before and after medical procedures. All patients were prayed for by the pharmacists on their way out of the hospital.

The City of Faith took the matter of prayer seriously. However, there was much conflict that administrators and staff had to deal with. Although continuing education efforts and orientation to the new philosophy of medical practice were available, the new way of practicing medicine was incredibly challenging to some physicians. Used to being in charge, working with the healing teams was exceedingly difficult for them. Sometimes heated arguments took place in interdisciplinary staff (healing team) meetings. I recall a doctor banging the table and shouting, "I am the healing team."

Oral Roberts put his money where his mouth was concerning spiritual care. At one point, the budget for the spiritual care department—which included clinical chaplains called "staff prayer partners" (making prayer the main work of chaplains by design) and professional counselors—approached $1 million. I began work as a staff prayer partner with an office on the first floor of the City of Faith, working with patients in the medical-surgical unit. I also worked from time to time with the oncology patients, psychiatric patients, and family practice patients. There were some well-known charismatic clergy serving as chaplains in our department. The spiritual care staff was multi-denominational, and all were committed to Oral Roberts' theology of healing. Dr. Stan Beason was a Methodist pastor from Alabama. Dr. Roy Pike and Dr. Gene Koelker were Methodist pastors from Maine. Dr. David Dunning was an ordained Disciples of Christ pastor and a retired Navy chaplain from the Northwest. David Wakefield, who later earned his doctorate and became a psychologist, was a Pentecostal prayer partner. I was considered a junior member of the staff along with many others.

There was a large lay chaplains' training program at the City of Faith—led by Dr. Stan Beason—which produced some outstanding lay caregivers from the greater Tulsa area who made the staff chaplains' life much easier, as we were trying to actively cover the hospital around the clock. Lay members from churches were recruited and screened carefully and were given substantive classroom training and practical clinical experience. Those who completed the training were certified to work with the staff prayer partners and they visited patients, offering pastoral care and referrals to staff ministers when needed. These outstanding lay ministers sacrificially offered themselves to serve the patients who came from various parts of the world. One of those outstanding caregivers who lived in Jenks, Oklahoma, Carole Burk, became a lifelong friend to us.

The City of Faith had a field education program involving students from ORU Seminary. Later, a nationally recognized CPE program was also established. Rev. Herbert Hillebrand, a former president of the College of Chaplains (now Association of Professional Chaplains), was hired as the CPE supervisor. Rev. Kenneth Blank, another CPE supervisor with a Presbyterian background, was added and CPE was offered to both students of the ORU Seminary and selected staff prayer partners. I was able to complete two additional units of CPE with the Rev. Hillebrand, adding to the four units I had completed at Norwich Hospital.

## College of Chaplains Honors Oral Roberts

The College of Chaplains (now Association of Professional Chaplains) has been the premier association of professional chaplains in the United States. This group took notice of what was happening at the City of Faith, seeing the size of the staff and the investment Oral Roberts was making in spiritual care, as well as the revolutionary idea of merging medicine and prayer, which made chaplains full and active professional members of the medical care teams. This was a novel idea in the 1980s. Although television evangelists were not usually involved with professional associations such as the College of Chaplains, Oral Roberts was invited to be the keynote speaker at the annual conference of the association in 1983. I was fortunate to attend that conference in San Diego and hear Oral Roberts speak about his philosophy of whole person medicine and the efforts he was making at the City of Faith. I was certified as a Fellow in the College of Chaplains (now known as Board Certified Chaplain) formally at that conference, having completed all the requirements by then.

Rev. David Dunning was my immediate supervisor in the hospital. He enrolled in the Doctor of Ministry program at Oral Roberts University in 1982, and I followed him in 1983, both with employee tuition assistance. I graduated in 1986. My applied research project was titled, "A clinical model of pastoral ministry to persons in chronic pain." After my graduation, I was appointed as the associate director for training for the Department of Spiritual Care. This was a position first held by Dr. Stan Beason and later by Dr. Gene Koelker. Eventually I was promoted to be the associate director for administration for the chaplaincy department of the division called Spiritual Care Services. Spiritual Care Services was divided into two departments—the pastoral care department consisting of the staff chaplains (prayer partners) and the counseling department consisting of the professional counselors. Dr. Duie Jernigan remained the leader for the whole division, and I reported to him. During this period, I served as an adjunct faculty (called clinical faculty) at the seminary, teaching pastoral care courses and working with the field education program.

I was fortunate to assist Dr. Gene Koelker as he taught a required course for the fourth-year medical students at ORU. Called Healing Team Concepts, this was a course co-taught by a medical doctor and a teaching chaplain to prepare ORU medical school students to work as whole person healers with sufficient theological orientation and preparation to work with healing teams. Dr. Gene Koelker was a person of great knowledge and wisdom. I learned much from him, clinically and academically, that helped me to take his place to teach the medical students with Dr. Roger Youmans, MD after he retired from the City of Faith and returned to Maine. The things I learned from Dr. Koelker helped me when I entered the seminary later as professor of pastoral care.

Dr. Jernigan used to invite the entire staff with their families to his house where he and his wife Norma treated us to great times of food, fellowship, and celebration. I learned much regarding ministry and leadership from him. He had a great impact on me and my family as he modeled true mentoring. For example, after I graduated with a Doctor of Ministry from Oral Roberts University, he kept encouraging me to think about getting another doctorate and becoming a full-time professor in the seminary. He went out of his way and wrote to the few universities that were offering accredited nontraditional doctorates in counseling (in those days almost all doctoral programs offered only residential format) and made me look at those catalogs carefully to see what might work in my situation. He also encouraged Molly to pursue her registered nurse license in Oklahoma. She followed his counsel and got licensed as a registered nurse and worked for thirty years as a medical surgical nurse at St. Francis Hospital in Tulsa.

In 1988, while I was still at the City of Faith, I began taking classes for the Doctor of Education in Adult Education with a focus in Counseling in the traditional doctoral program at Oklahoma State University in Stillwater, Oklahoma. I started the program with much hesitation, not knowing if I could commute that far for four years to finish the work with a full-time job that was quite demanding. With God's help, I completed the EdD degree in 1992. I was fortunate to get permission to do research and write a dissertation on the post-MDiv learning needs of ministers/chaplains, which produced new information on how to develop research-based DMin curriculums. I was able to publish the findings in academic journals.

[One such article can be downloaded freely at: https://digitalshowcase.oru.edu/sotl_ched/vol5/iss1/2/ ]

I remain grateful to Dr. Jernigan. Jernigan had an impact not only on me and Molly, but also on our children. Many years after he left the City of Faith to start a private counseling practice, Jamie invited him and his wife to her house and we joined them for a wonderful dinner and an unforgettable time of fellowship and reminiscing. (Thanks, Jamie.)

My secretary during the time of service as a staff prayer partner was Ms. Sheree King, a young woman with a sterling character and superior people skills. Years later, she earned her doctorate from ORU School of Education and served as the university registrar. A nurse I worked with at the City of Faith, Kenda Jezek, later became the dean of the nursing school at ORU. Working at the City of Faith was a life-transforming experience for most of us who were involved in such a pioneering effort.

## City of Faith Closes

Although the vision of the City of Faith was historic, that project could not be sustained economically. The institution struggled to attract enough patients to support it financially. There were also many other challenges. Moreover, the great scandals involving televangelists during the 1980s, although Oral Roberts was not personally involved in them, affected the Oral Roberts Ministry. [Oral's statement that "God will call me home" if he did not receive 8 million dollars became a controversy, but those of us who heard it on campus knew that Oral was trying to raise the money to give 100 percent tuition scholarships to medical students to persuade them to go to serve in a mission field, foreign or domestic, for the number of years they received free medical education. He had noticed that medical graduates were not going on missions due to their heavy student debts.] Due to these and other reasons, the City of Faith was closed in 1989 and the ORU School of Medicine as well as ORU School of Dentistry also were closed. ORU's law school library was given to Regent University in Virginia.

## Move to ORU Seminary

When Dr. Duie Jernigan resigned his position and started a private counseling practice in Tulsa, I was told that I was being considered to replace him as director of the Spiritual Care Services. During this period, I received an unexpected call from Dr. Paul Chappell who was dean of the ORU Seminary at that time (following Dr. Jimmy Buskirk and Rev. Larry Lea). He told me that earlier in the day he felt impressed to offer me the position of dean of students, director of field education, and professor of pastoral care in the Seminary. The position at the City of Faith vacated by Dr. Jernigan had much better salary and benefits than the position I was being offered at the Seminary which involved both teaching and administrative responsibilities year-round. I decided to ask my father-in-law, Rev. K. J. George, who was visiting us from India at that time to pray for us and guide us in this choice. He spent some time praying in the guest room of our house and came down to tell me to take the position with the lower pay. I obeyed him and accepted the academic position. Two weeks after that decision, it was announced that Oral Roberts University was closing its medical school and the affiliated City of Faith Medical and Research Center. Hundreds of people lost their jobs and many of them thought that I had inside information to move to the University in a timely fashion. The truth is that I was just following Papa's advice and had no idea that they were considering closing the City of Faith.

This was really a new beginning in my life. I was a student in the Doctor of Education program at Oklahoma State University during the first 3 years of my service as professor and dean of students in the seminary. They were tough years in terms of balancing the demands of the work, keeping up with my homework, doing a major research study for the dissertation, and balancing my schedule with Molly's schedule as a nurse, keeping up with travels for the university and responding to invitations to preach nationally.

I had many opportunities during this period to learn the tricks of the trade in academic administration as I was fortunate to be involved in the operation of the seminary under Dr. Paul Chappell, a no-nonsense dean who demanded excellence from everyone including himself. Additionally, I was mentored by the director (called dean in those days) of the DMin program, Dr. Charles Snow, who had replaced Dr. Ed Wimberly in that position who moved to the Interdenominational Theological Center in Atlanta where he later became president. [Mrs. Mary Ellen Snow was my last secretary at the City of Faith.] Dr. Snow got me involved in the national meetings of the directors of DMin programs which later became the Association for DMin Education (ADME). I was fortunate to be with him at the annual meeting in Chicago when ADME was formally organized and both of us became charter members. Before coming to ORU, Dr. Snow and Dr. Kenneth Mayton, chairman of the undergraduate department of Theology, were associates of Rev. David Wilkerson, founder of the restoration and rehabilitation ministry, Teen Challenge. Dr. Snow decided to resign his position and accept a pastorate in Fort Worth, and I was appointed to lead the DMin program. I really enjoyed that work but did not get to stay in that position for long.

## Jerry Horner and the Tom and Jerry Show

ORU Seminary had an extension at Church on the Way, a church belonging to the International Foursquare Gospel Church, in Van Nuys, California where Dr. Jack Hayford was pastor. As that extension became The King's Seminary, an independent theological institution, Dr. Paul Chappell became its chief academic officer and moved to California.

## A Seminary Dean's Experiment with Servant Leadership

Dr. Jerry Horner replaced him as Seminary Dean at ORU. Dr. Horner who was a professor in the Theology department at ORU earlier had been invited to become the founding dean of the seminary at Regent University. After that school was well established, Dr. Horner decided to return to ORU. He was teaching in the undergraduate department of Theology when Dr. Chappell left. When he became dean, I was asked to serve as the associate dean for academic affairs. I left the DMin office and began serving in this new role.

Dr. Jerry Horner was a pastoral leader who wanted an associate to take care of the daily administrative details. He had a gentle spirit and much experience working with the accrediting association—the Association of Theological Schools in the United States and Canada (ATS)—which was a great asset to the seminary at that time. Before he left, Dr. Chappell had started several worthy projects. For instance, under his direction we had started an extension program in North Tulsa for African American pastors in Oklahoma. We also began offering courses in Oklahoma City for the pastors who found the distance between Oklahoma City and North Tulsa too far. These were in addition to the extension site in Van Nuys. Dr. Horner's experience with the ATS proved useful in redistributing the seminary's energies. Dr. Horner invited Dr. Dan Alshire, who at that time was the ATS liaison for ORU, to come to Tulsa and examine our situation to offer counsel. Dan, a gracious man who became the director of ATS later for a long period of time, was immensely helpful to us in sorting out our situation and properly consolidating our extension sites.

I was considered an ideal administrative partner for Dr. Horner as I had some gifts in paying attention to details. Our colleagues called our administration the Tom and Jerry show. I enjoyed working with Dr. Horner as he turned out to be a kind and good mentor for me, helping me to learn the ways of the ATS. We attended ATS conferences together where he introduced me to his friends who were deans of other seminaries. I also enjoyed traveling with Dr. Horner to ATS conferences and on one occasion, to Myanmar on an unforgettable ministry trip.

## Becoming Dean of the ORU Seminary

One day during the 1999 fall semester, I received a call from Dr. Frank Hultgren (a friend of President Richard Roberts who served as faculty chaplain) telling me to expect an important call from the president. He said enough to let me know that a major change was coming. I was really surprised when I received that call from President Richard Roberts and learned that Dr. Horner was finishing his term and that he had decided to appoint me as the next dean of the seminary. He told me that his father, Chancellor Oral Roberts, had already approved my appointment. Later I learned from Richard and his wife Lindsay that years earlier while I was still at the City of Faith, Oral had told them to keep an eye on me for a leadership position in the seminary. I remembered Provost Carl Hamilton telling me once that I did not have enough gray hair yet to become dean. I learned that I would become dean on January 1, 2000.

I did not expect to become the next dean and I did not believe I was fully qualified to be the head of the theological

## A Seminary Dean's Experiment with Servant Leadership

school at ORU. Stereotypically, Indians in America are scientists, not Christian theologians. I had mixed feelings about the appointment because I genuinely enjoyed being the associate dean, not having all the attention and headaches of leadership but getting to do academic administration and some teaching and being connected with all the outreaches of the seminary. But on the first day of the year 2000, at the age of 48, I became the fifth dean of the seminary at Oral Roberts University, following Dr. James Buskirk, Rev. Larry Lea, Dr. Paul Chappell, and Dr. Jerry Horner. Although the faculty was very supportive, I was unsure of my future as dean at ORU as I was following two very experienced leaders. I was relieved that I had taken some advice from Dr. Chappell a few years earlier. He had advised me to apply for tenure before applying for full professorship. He had told me that it was a good thing for administrators as one could go back to teaching if administration did not work out. I had followed his advice and had become tenured before I became a full professor!

As a result of a change made by the university when Dr. Chappell left, the undergraduate theology department at ORU was not associated with the graduate seminary. The undergraduate theology program was a department in the School of Arts and Sciences, reporting to Dean George Thyvelikakath, a scientist from India. All the colleges were called schools in those days and since then the School of Arts and Sciences has become two separate colleges at the university. A decision was made when I became dean to bring the undergraduate theology program back to the School of Theology and Ministry under my supervision.

The School of Theology and Ministry had a well-respected faculty on campus. Men and women with outstanding credentials, impeccable character, and diverse ministerial experiences taught in the undergraduate and graduate levels of the school. They represented multiple denominations—United Methodist, Baptist, United Church of Christ, Assemblies of God, Church of God (Cleveland), etc.—and independent charismatic churches. All were serious followers of Jesus Christ who were committed to a Pentecostal/charismatic theological perspective, well aware of the nuances of the differences between classical Pentecostals and charismatics. Under the direction of the university president and dean, they gave spiritual leadership to the campus in several areas. Reciting the history of the divinity schools at Harvard and Yale, Oral Roberts had told us again and again to guard the seminary theologically. He had said, "As the seminary goes, so goes the university." The faculty and I took Oral's exhortation seriously. When I became dean, there was a campus-wide sense that the theology faculty was outstanding.

## A Word about Whole Person Education

Oral Roberts developed the whole person education philosophy considering wholeness as a biblical concept. This philosophy implemented in all the colleges of ORU had its roots in his healing ministry that was based on the biblical idea of wholeness as seen in 1 Thessalonians 5:23:

"Now may the God of peace Himself sanctify you completely; and may your whole spirit, soul, and body be preserved blameless at the coming of our Lord Jesus Christ."

Oral believed that education should not deal with intellectual development alone but must intentionally involve the student's body and spirit also. He believed that students need more than academic learning. They must develop physically through a required custom-designed aerobic program and must advance spiritually through monitored worship and discipleship experiences. The faculty developed five learning outcomes based on these assumptions. Accordingly, an ORU education must prepare the graduates to be global citizens who are (1) Spiritually Alive, (2) Intellectually Alert, (3) Physically Disciplined, (4) Socially Adept, and (5) Professionally Competent. There is a robust assessment program in place involving all levels of ORU to make sure that these goals are accomplished. The accrediting associations hold ORU accountable to these stated goals. One cannot graduate from ORU by just passing the traditional academic courses. All students are required to attend chapel services regularly and formally pass personally adapted aerobic courses.

## The "So What?" Committee

One of the first things I did as dean was to appoint a committee called the 21$^{st}$ century theological education committee. I appointed Dr. Ed Decker as the chair of the committee and appointed professors from each area of the curriculum and an equal number of pastors from the community as members. The pastors represented small churches, mega churches, white churches, and nonwhite churches. I commissioned the committee to study what type of theological education would be required for effective ministry in the 21st century. Normally, academic committees involve faculty persons, basically PhD's, only. I wanted to know what professors could learn from the pastors and how pastors could influence the curriculum. I knew that across the world, academia and the church were in two different planes, and I was hoping to do something to minimize the big gulf between the two because I was sick of hearing some people, particularly in the Pentecostal/charismatic tradition, calling all seminaries cemeteries.

Dr. Decker's committee was an excellent work group that labored for a year and produced a report that significantly impacted both teaching and learning at Oral Roberts University College of Theology and Ministry. The committee's report was brought to the faculty, and we had professional development sessions to review every course, every degree program, every program/course objective, and the mission of the school itself, ultimately, in its light. We looked at every syllabus with the question: so what? We had outstanding scholars teaching excellent courses, but we chose to ask the "so what?" question to scrutinize ourselves in terms of our mission. World-class scholars who taught the traditional courses faced questions like these in a supportive environment: in a seminary built "to impact the world with God's healing," how will this course help students who are called to be scholars and at the same time contribute to prepare other students who are called to professional ministry in multiple contexts? How will this course benefit the church and the people of God? How will it help to fulfill the purposes of God in the world? Initially the questions seemed threatening, but as the faculty tried to connect their teaching to the mission of the school, this became the most profitable time we spent together. I do not know how many deans would dare to do this or be allowed to do this, but in an atmosphere without threat and intimidation, the professors took the challenge seriously and the school and its students benefited.

This exercise resulted in significant changes in the curriculum and changed the way we were teaching our courses. Some professors struggled more than others, and we had arguments and discussions—but in a loving atmosphere where my approach was to allow them total freedom to agree or disagree and "fight it out," several wonderful things happened. I will share just one example from the church history course. Dr. David Dorries, who was teaching the church history course, changed one of his major assignments for the course. Instead of asking for a paper on some historical event in church history regarding time and place and people as usual, he asked the MDiv students (professional ministry students) to study the history and apply that history in their places of ministry and come up with a product that would show that they understood the history, learned from the history, and were able to implement something in their ministry based on that learning.

For example, Dorries asked students in a class on the Reformation to study the reformers, particularly Martin Luther and his teachings on justification by faith, to develop sermons based on the theological themes of the Reformation, preach those in their churches or ministries, and submit a summary of their learning as well as the outlines of sermons they preached, along with an evaluation of the whole experience. Students really learned church history but in a new way to benefit the ministry of the church. Of course, we had academic programs like MA degrees in Biblical Literature, Advanced Languages, Theology, etc., where students needed to study the Bible, its languages and cognates, theology, and church history in a traditional, scholarly way. They were given corresponding ways to seek lasting outcomes of their learning. But in Master of Divinity and other graduate professional degrees, the students were forced to think about what they were learning and how that was preparing them for a more excellent ministry that would be well informed, professional, and guided by the Holy Spirit.

Those were exciting days. I remain grateful to Dr. Ed Decker, a very smart colleague, who was well-liked by his peers and who had the energy to keep a lively discussion going in the committee and with the faculty for a whole year.

## Fast-Track MA and DMin Programs

ORU Seminary grew in multiple ways during this period. We had already begun new creative programs when Dr. Horner was dean as distance education was beginning to develop in ATS seminaries. The modular program started by Dr. Chappell was already successful under the leadership of Dr. Lillian Breckenridge. [Tech savvy Dr. James Tollett assisted us to launch our way into distance education.] I decided to invest extra energy in the so-called Fast-Track programs and the international programs. The charismatic movement was in its heyday as storefront churches were becoming mega churches. These churches were grooming their ministry staff through their own Bible institutes. Many of the senior pastors who taught at these institutes lacked any type of formal theological education. We saw the need for theological education everywhere in the movement, but many leaders were against higher education in theology. Many mega churches and major ministries were connected to the Oral and Richard Roberts ministries, and we wanted to draw them to the seminary.

We designed an MA program first and later a DMin program to attract these pastors and leaders to pursue theological education. The programs were branded as Fast-Track, but each program was the traditional modular curriculum made more user-friendly in terms of scheduled time on campus (not reduced residency time, but timing that was sensitive to church calendars) and selection of participants. We created peer groups of people with larger ministries who were more open to joining a program of study with others who were dealing with ministry issues particular to larger charismatic mega churches and organizations. They had to take the same number of courses as other students in these degree programs. In many cases their churches and ministries paid their school bills. Classes were held in a conference room on the sixth floor of the Graduate Center where university deans' offices were located, not on the fourth floor where the regular seminary classes were held. In fact, we added a premium to their fees in the DMin class and offered refreshments and catered daily lunches in the classroom. (Some students commuted to campus in their own airplanes! It was interesting to hear them compare their planes during some breaks!) The Fast-Track degrees were modeled after the executive MBA degree. [There was real discomfort about the elite image of the Fast-Track cohorts, but the desperate need for biblically sound theology in the charismatic movement trumped the concern.]

Several well-known charismatic pastors and leaders joined our programs and successfully completed both the MA and DMin Fast-Track degrees. Richard Roberts, our president, joined the pioneer Fast-Track DMin group which included Bishop Michael Reid from Peniel Pentecostal Church in England, Billy Joe Daugherty, pastor of Victory Christian Center, a mega church in Tulsa, and several others of similar caliber. Having to teach the president of the university was a challenge to our professors, but he was a model student in the classroom, missing not one session during the years of course work. He was teaching a course titled "Signs and Wonders" that was required for all ORU students. His DMin dissertation studied the impact of this course on the students in terms of their knowledge, attitude, and practice of signs and wonders. Dr. Dan Thimell served as his project advisor.

I had some interesting experiences during this time. For instance, one day I was in the president's office with the provost complaining about the lower funding of the school of theology despite the revenue we were generating. I did not get much help. On the same day in the afternoon the president was in the DMin class complaining about the length of the post-course paper that was required in the course! He did not get a break either. President Richard Roberts submitted all his papers within the deadlines.

It was an exciting sight to see these mega church pastors and leaders of well-known ministries dealing with academic matters and arguing about theological principles and practical issues related to ministry. Teaching this group was a challenge to all the professors involved. I taught them some courses, but our typical curriculum required all the regular teachers. Knowing the risk of putting all DMin faculty in this class which included the university's president and others considered by many as VIP's, we selected professors with better diplomatic skills to teach the courses. I remember one professor hesitating to go into that class and later struggling with the class as some students were not open to certain academic ideas he was sharing. He was much appreciated at the end of the course but had to deal with difficult responses from some students initially. I invited a well-known expert to teach a course. This highly accomplished academic leader taught a particular class in which he shared some statistics from research regarding certain evangelistic efforts. Some pastors in the classroom had a difficult time with the data he shared, and it created some extra tension in the class. I had to intervene as dean to bring peace to the class.

Educators know that it is not uncommon for students to have cognitive dissonance as new information comes to them that contradicts their prior knowledge or belief. Normally those lead to meaningful discussions that help the students and end well in most cases. But when you have leaders of large ministries and mega churches in an academic class, there is a different dynamic. For instance, at moments of dissonance, instead of dealing with the data and dialoging, one student used to stand up, turn toward the wall, and start speaking in tongues, holding up his hands. From his conversations, it became clear that he had a real fear that through unsuspecting academic thoughts, the devil could enter his spirit and plant doubts and destroy his large ministry.

I had to pay extra attention to the Fast-Track group's classes, teachers, student feedback, and the academic demands of an earned doctorate. Sometimes I sat in the class as other professors taught. Thankfully, we were able to keep the standards and everyone in the first cohort completed the course work, wrote noticeable dissertations, and graduated. Others whose ministries were significantly impacted by subsequent cohorts of the Fast-Track DMin program include such leaders as Dennis Lindsay and his daughter Missy Lindsay of Christ for the Nations, Dallas; and Steve Stells, founding pastor of the House of Prayer Church in Chesterfield, Virginia.

*Chapter 4*

# A Seminary Serving the World

## International Academic Programs

Dr. Paul Chappell was a visionary. He had started a Doctor of Ministry program for pastors from Korea. This was initiated in response to a request from Dr. Yeol Soo Eim, president of the Foursquare Gospel Theological Seminary in Taejon, South Korea, and encouraged by Pastor Jack Hayford of Van Nyes, California, who had denominational connections with the Korean seminary. Working with Provost Carl Hamilton, Dr. Chappell also had initiated an outreach to a school related to the Livets Ord (Living Word) Church led by Rev. Ulf Ekman in Uppsala, Sweden. [ORU School of Education also developed a program at Livets Ord University (LOU).] I was part of the planning of the theology program in Korea and Sweden. We also had a relationship with Peniel College in Essex, England, which was connected to Peniel Pentecostal Church pastored by Bishop Michael Reid. We had two of our professors—Dr. Roy Hayden and Dr. Sam Thorpe—serve at Peniel as resident teachers and deans at different times.

Technically we had what was called sister agreements with these schools. The dean of the Livets Ord Seminary, Dr. Anders Gerdmar, was an outstanding scholar and a gentle shepherd. The president of the Korean seminary, Dr. Yeol Soo Eim, was a highly gifted leader and a graduate of Fuller Theological Seminary. Through his efforts the Korean school acquired a beautiful new campus, developed degrees all the way to PhD, gained an excellent reputation, and national accreditation, partially strengthened by its relationship with Oral Roberts University. When we went to Korea first to teach at that school, we taught in classes in the basement of an old building, wearing heavy coats while lecturing during winter months. Dr. Eim was able to build a modern campus there.

The Foursquare Gospel denomination in Korea was pioneered by an American-educated female pastor who was known to everyone as Sister Ahn who was a refugee from North Korea. She had founded a multi-campus high school with a great reputation for academic quality and character development of students in Taejon. It was only natural for a college connected with her ministry to become a strong institution of theological education.

Dr. Eim, while serving as the president of the seminary in Korea worked closely with the DMin director (then dean of doctoral studies) at ORU and served concurrently as the director of the Korean DMin program. Korean pastors in the DMin program spent about five weeks on ORU

## A Seminary Dean's Experiment with Servant Leadership

campus taking their courses during the summer for two years, completed their applied research projects during the following years at their places of ministry in Korea, and returned to campus for graduation. In the beginning, mostly two groups of pastors from Korea came during the summer: ministers from various denominations in Korea (Baptist, Methodist, Presbyterian, etc.) including pastors belonging to the Foursquare Gospel Church as one group and another group from Pastor Paul Yonggi Cho's Yoido Full Gospel Church, the largest church in the world. Sometimes there were dynamic disagreements between these two groups regarding doctrines and church polity while they were on our campus. Sometimes, Dr. Eim and the seminary leaders had to intervene as diplomatic peacemakers.

This pioneering program took considerable planning by the seminary leadership team and Dr. Eim and upper level ORU administrators who were unfamiliar with the intricacies of such an international program. We had to plan the courses, teachers, translators, bilingual textbooks, student workers, airport pick-ups, currency conversion, jet lag considerations, aerobic classes, bilingual chapel services, welcome parties, special lunches, Korean pastors' desire to see America, and their desire to do mall shopping that they considered cheap, and we had to do all this in a profitable way for ORU. Imagine working with the upper administrators and ORU Chief Financial Officers who had nothing like this happening in any other school without alienating them! It took the tireless and sacrificial efforts of a faithful faculty, staff, and administrators in the seminary to make this happen successfully.

Dr. Brad Young is an eminent scholar who was one of several ORU graduates who returned after their doctoral studies elsewhere to teach at their alma mater. [Dr. Young received his PhD from Hebrew University in Jerusalem. During a visit to Israel, I was surprised to notice a tour bus driver reading Dr. Young's book, *Jesus the Jewish Theologian*!] He was very instrumental in growing the Korean DMin program. The Korean pastors were having trouble getting student visas from the US embassy in Seoul in the beginning because of their unusual summer-only residential study in the US. We wrote to the embassy explaining the unusual nature of our doctoral program for pastors from Korea, but it was the purposeful support and outreaches of Dr. Young's father, former Oklahoma State Senator John W. Young, that loosened the red tape at the embassy. Later, the Young family welcomed each Korean DMin cohort into their home in Sapulpa with a celebratory picnic during July 4th weekends. Every year, these gatherings ended with the whole group of Americans and Koreans in the Young family's beautiful backyard singing out loud with accompaniments the beloved song "God bless, America" first, and then, "God bless Korea," substituting only the name of the country! This was one of the highlights of our Korean students' summer trips to Tulsa.

ORU Seminary professors were sent to each international location to offer classes in rotation. I recall going to Van Nuys to coteach a pastoral care course with Pastor Jack Hayford. It was a wonderful experience. I also remember being thrown off a hotel bed in Van Nyes during the aftershock of a major earthquake. Those were challenging times for all seminary professors, especially the administrators. While these programs brought new students and additional revenue, there was no extra reward for the teachers and staff involved in this effort. This was our service to God and His work in the world. We knew that we were fulfilling the mission of ORU and were providing badly needed theological education to the churches and ministries within the Pentecostal/charismatic movement.

With the goal of eventually making the LOU Theological Seminary in Sweden an official extension of our seminary with the approval of ATS, I worked with that school to start not only an MA program but also an MDiv program. Their initial interest was only in a European-model MA degree, but we were able to convince them of the usefulness of an MDiv as both an academic and professional degree that would have a better impact on their students and their future evangelistic and pastoral ministries in Europe. ORU professors kept flying to Uppsala, Sweden and teaching modular courses there. It was a pleasure for Molly and me to go there several times to teach. I kept the ATS informed of our collaborative work in Sweden, stating that it was a missionary effort of our faculty with the hope that someday it would become an officially approved extension site for us. I informed the ATS that we were keeping all the ATS standards there already without claiming that the Livets Ord graduate program was a formal part of ORU.

## More on Korea

Dr. Yeol Soo Eim was a highly energetic leader. He was a well-known pastor, theological educator, and in addition to being the president of Foursquare Gospel Theological Seminary in Taejon, he was also the president of the Society for Pentecostal Studies in Korea. As the denominational name of his school became a problem for some of its graduates to be employed in certain places in Asia, the school's name was changed to Asia Life University (ALU). Dr. Eim was a protégé of Mrs. Ahn who trusted him with the school. Sister Ahn had a son, Sam, who followed her as pastor of the Foursquare Gospel church in Taejon, the mother church of the school and the denomination. His wife Sarah was a brilliant scholar who had earned her PhD in England. She did an outstanding job teaching at Asia Life. Dr. Eim, Sarah, and others translated for us when we taught. We had special permission from ATS to teach the Korean DMin program in the Korean language with only the thesis translated into English at the end. We also required translations of sample papers from the courses to monitor the quality of the students' academic work and hired Korean-speaking adjunct faculty to evaluate all papers.

I made several trips to Korea recruiting pastors while traveling and preaching with Dr. Eim across the country. Molly accompanied me on many of these trips. When I was the director of the Doctor of Ministry program, I used to go there to conduct DMin comprehensive exams. Later when I became dean, when Molly and I made the trips to Korea together, Dr. Eim, accompanied by others, took us to tour different parts of the country, including the historic Demilitarized Zone (DMZ) and the beautiful Jeju Island. Our Korean hosts were truly kind to us and left us with very fond memories of many people and places in that beautiful land.

## A Seminary Dean's Experiment with Servant Leadership

At one time I was invited to speak at the Korean Air Force chapel where one of our graduates was a chaplain. I had helped him with his DMin dissertation which dealt with the death anxiety Korean military personnel had to deal with under the constant threat from North Korea. I preached in the Air Force chapel and had a formal dinner with Dr. Eim and several officers in the exclusive Generals' Dining Room. It was an interesting experience in that my plate had seven forks on the left and seven knives on the right, and other utensils to handle a seven-course dinner.

During these trips I had the privilege of preaching at Yoido Full Gospel Church. I also had opportunities to visit Rev. Yonggi Cho at his residence. Dr. Vinson Synan was with me and Dr. Eim during one of the visits. Both Dr. Synan and I presented papers on Dr. Cho's theology of healing at an academic conference held at Hansei University where Mrs. Cho, an ORU DMin graduate, was president. We visited her at her office one day. Rev. Choi, another ORU DMin graduate, was the number two leader in the pastoral ministries team at Yoido. He was a great host. I will never forget preaching in the main sanctuary at Yoido from a balcony-like platform that was about 35 steps above the pastor's office, looking at thousands of faces and knowing that many more thousands were watching in different locations, and being translated into multiple languages. Dr. Eim has always been an outstanding translator from English to Korean. In classrooms and in pulpits, he communicated in a beautiful and powerful way, staying right with my energy and tone as I spoke. God moved in a wonderful way in the services at Yoido.

Many of our DMin graduates are pastoring large Methodist, Presbyterian, Pentecostal, and other congregations in Korea. Five of them became bishops in the Methodist Church. There was no shortage of invitations for us to speak at these churches, but we were not able to go everywhere. We did visit several churches, from Seoul to Pusan, and were pleased to see what God was doing through our graduates. I also preached twice at the annual healing conference organized by ORU DMin alumni, which was held at Yoido's prayer mountain. It was so rewarding to see the pastors who sat in the ORU classrooms and later struggled to write their dissertations now leading such great ministries, preaching the gospel, baptizing people, and doing international missions and charity work. It was simply a pleasure to see the outcome of the work of ORU Seminary faculty and staff across South Korea. Some of our Korean graduates are doing missionary work in China and more discreetly in North Korea. I will not mention their methods here, but I can testify that as a result of their ministry, we now have many followers of Jesus and brothers and sisters in Christ in Kim Jong-un's North Korea.

## Sweden and Singapore

ORU's relationship with the Swedish seminary was a strong one with much anticipation regarding it becoming an official extension of ORU Seminary. It was a great surprise when we heard that the founder of the Livets Ord ministry, Ulf Ekman, had decided to become a Roman Catholic and abdicate his pastoral position at the church in Uppsala. He was studying the history of the Church, particularly the history of the Catholic church, and was living in Israel for a while.

I recalled the times when we had conversations regarding Livets Ord and his relationship with Oral Roberts. He had been to my office at ORU and told me the story of how Livets Ord started. He once visited the ORU campus and was sitting in a car in the parking lot of Mabee Center, looking at the prayer tower. He sensed the voice of God in his heart saying to him, "Everything you see here came to being because of the faith of one man – Oral Roberts. If you would return to your homeland and believe me, I will give you a ministry like this." Livets Ord became such a ministry in a spiritually unfriendly culture.

Ulf Ekman had a church with 2,000 members when the nearest cathedral, so impressive in structure and standing, had only about 35 people attending worship services on Sundays. I have preached at his church and gave the commencement address at a graduation ceremony held in the church building. I had met with him privately and had long conversations with him during my visits to Uppsala. His wife had grown up in India as her parents were missionaries there. I was really shocked when I heard about Ekman's abdication. His conversion caused a great fall away at the church and it has not fully recovered. The Livets Ord University had to be closed. With much effort and sacrifices made by Dr. Anders Gerdmar, a new seminary was formed with the name Scandinavian School of Theology. Gerdmar is its president.

The formal relationship between Livets Ord and ORU came to an end. The Scandinavian School of Theology signed a sister agreement or entered into a similar relationship with Southeastern University in Lakeland, Florida where Dr. Rutland served as president prior to his tenure at Oral Roberts University. Dr. Rutland assisted Gerdmar to establish this relationship and he checked with me regarding the nature and history of ORU's relationship with LOU before finalizing the new relationship with Southeastern. Dr. Gerdmar stayed in touch with me all through the years, communicating with me and giving me updates about the status of the new school. Although the school is functioning well, the existing contextual problems of Christian schools in Sweden still afflict the seminary. A true scholar, a gentle soul, and a sincere man of God, Anders Gerdmar has done an outstanding job as president in an exceedingly difficult situation. I consider it a privilege to know him and thank God for his life and ministry, and for his family.

One of the most beautiful cities Molly and I have visited is Stockholm, Sweden. During one of our visits, Dr. Anders Gerdmar and his wife Else-Marie took us to Stockholm and gave us an elaborate tour of the city. Swedish people affectionately call Stockholm the city between water and heaven. We saw the beautiful parts of the city and many institutions, including the royal palace. The most unforgettable visit was to the Nobel Prize Museum in the city. We saw the displays regarding the various recipients of the Nobel Prize throughout the years and saw the items related to the life of Rabindranath Tagore, the Indian Nobel laureate. A description of his life and the reasons for his selection were presented there. Dr. Gerdmar and Else-Marie took us to some special eating places for lunch and dinner, uniquely Swedish places with distinctive features in terms of seating, atmosphere, and food. We will never forget those times.

Closing an accredited extension program in a foreign country is not an easy task. As the undergraduate theology program at LOU in Uppsala was approved by the American regional accrediting association, the Higher Learning Commission (HLC), as an extension program, ORU was obligated to make sure that arrangements were made for current students in the program to complete their degrees in some way at ORU or another institution. ORU decided to allow students to complete their undergraduate degrees by taking online courses from ORU. Much work went into this by the registrar's office in both locations to identify the students, their level of progress in the degree program, and their ability to take online courses at ORU. Most students completed their degrees this way.

As the graduate theological program at Livets Ord was not an official extension program approved by the ATS yet, we had no legal obligation to assist those students with the closing of their school. However, I felt morally obligated to help the students in the master's program in Sweden. In searching for a way to help the students complete their graduate degrees at our seminary, I found that most of them had come to Sweden for this degree from one church in Singapore. There was another student who was in that program from Faroe Island, an island in the northern Atlantic, south of Iceland. By then ORU had received approval to offer online graduate degrees and the ATS standards were moving in the direction of approving what is called blended courses. These are courses in which students do part of their academic work online and then meet in person to complete the courses. We were able to help these students to complete their degrees through our modular and distance education program. The student from Faroe Island joined his peers from Singapore and completed his degree.

The home church of our students in Singapore—the Heart of God Church—is a unique congregation in that it was basically a church for young people and by young people and is a mega church growing at a rapid rate. The average age of the leadership was less than 30 when we first visited the church. They have their own beautiful facility. Membership consists of mostly first-generation Christians who are mostly converts from Buddhism. Using cutting-edge technology and world-class music, they attract a great number of students. The senior pastors—Pastors Tan Seow How and Cecilia Chan—are outstanding leaders. They have been grooming a great team of associates who were the graduate students at Livets Ord. Charleston Lim and Garrett Lee are leaders among them, serving as senior associates to the pastors.

The church has special programs to increase fellowship and discipleship among young people, both students and professionals. They have afterschool programs for high school students that offer a safe place to study and socialize and at the same time grow in Christ. Both staff leaders and volunteers lead designated groups of young people to help them in their formation as followers of Christ.

The group of MDiv students from Singapore graduated as I was stepping down from deanship after 16 years, and it was our privilege to not only give them their degrees formally at the commencement on campus, but also to entertain the group at our house in Jenks. The student from Faroe Island—Bugvi Olsen—and his family from the island joined us at our house. All the graduates and their loved ones sat across the living room, family room, and kitchen, and ate broiled chicken and enjoyed Molly's peach cobbler. After the commencement, we traveled to Singapore and conducted a hooding ceremony in the church where those who supported their studies watched them receive their ORU degrees as I hooded them. By then I was former dean but was granted authority by the interim dean Dr. Sam Thorpe to conduct the ceremony in Singapore. It has been my privilege to preach and teach at Heart of God Church. Molly and I toured Kuala Lampur, Malaysia, during one of our trips to Singapore.

## The Czech Republic

I had the opportunity to preach and teach in the Czech Republic as a result of an invitation from the Livets Ord University and particularly from its dean, Pavel Hoffman, a native of the Czech Republic and a graduate of Oral Roberts University Seminary. He was involved in the translation of the Bible into his native language and was serving as the dean at Livets Ord. I traveled to the Czech Republic, preached at different churches, and taught a pastoral care course on behalf of Livets Ord University to students who had come from several European nations.

## With Livets Ord Team to Russia

Graduates of the Livets Ord school and their leaders had outreaches into the other countries of Europe and to Russia.

It was my privilege to go with them to Russia to conduct ministers' training seminars in Moscow where participants came from various parts of the country. At the time of our visit to Russia, conducting such a seminar was still considered a risky effort as the fall of the Soviet Union happened not long before that. I was told that some participants traveled for days by train to get to the seminar. Hundreds of people attended the sessions. I was accompanied by Dr. William Jernigan who was the dean of the Learning Resource Center and served as the ORU liaison for the undergraduate program in Sweden. Dr. J (as he was called) and I had gone to Sweden where I taught a graduate course and he represented ORU at their graduation. I gave the commencement address that year. In Russia, I taught several daytime seminar sessions and preached the gospel in the evenings, and joining others on the team, both Dr. Jernigan and I prayed for the Russian ministers lined up for prayer at the end of the services. Some days we stayed long into the night praying for these ministers. Dr. J told me that the experience reminded him of the Oral Roberts Ministries partner seminars held at ORU campus long ago.

## Faroe Island

Through ORU graduate Bugvi Olsen, I was invited to preach at a conference held at Keldan church in the Faroe Islands in April 2017. The Singaporean graduates with their pastor Lia Chan joined us there. The Heart of God Church conducts seminars across the world, teaching how to develop a church for young people. They did an outstanding job during the conference in the Faroe Island. I preached at several meetings and spoke at the seminar sessions. Our hosts took us around the island. We were told that some of the islands near the main island were very small but inhabited. One had only three or four people living on it. Someone joked that the population there was large enough to have a couple of Baptist churches!

Faroe Island is a beautiful place. We stayed in a guest house on the church campus, and it looked like we could see through the window more than one season in a single April day—spring rain, light winter snow, and summer sunshine. It was an unbelievable sight to see streams of water flowing down the mountains and the people said they could drink the water from the side of the street because pollution was practically nonexistent. They were doing everything they could to preserve it that way as tourism was beginning to affect the environment. We saw the place where they raise salmon in the ocean, creating a big business and one of the businessmen in the church was a major exporter. He was related to Bugvi. Our host church was the largest church on the main island. Rev. Pauli Hoj is a beloved pastor, and his wife Jastrid is a graduate of ORU College of Education.

The church leaders took us to private homes and tiny restaurants to feed us seafood and other unique meals. We were taken on an unforgettable trip to the capital, Torshavn, by Runi and Nomi Rasmussen. Runi was an assistant to the Prime Minister of the small island nation and a member of Keldan church. He gave us a tour of the Prime Minister's office and provided information on all the changes that have taken place in the capital building during its history. He had an interest in theology and we discussed the history of the Christian church in the island. We learned that the Pentecostal movement in this island had roots connected to Sweden similar to what Pentecostalism in Kerala had through Lewi Pethrus of Stockholm. I wrote an article about this history in the Malayalam Christian periodical *Good News*. We had lunch at a hotel where a suite is named after President Bill Clinton because he stayed in it during his first visit to the island.

The clean and clear water is what stays in our minds regarding this island along with the wonderful hospitality of the people there. In this small nation of less than 50,000 people, everyone seemed to know everyone else. God is at work in a big way in this small place.

Bugvi Olsen and his wife Birita have stayed connected with us and have kept us updated. They are serving God faithfully and their lovely family is growing. We also hear from the graduates in Singapore. They are all involved in God's work as their church is still growing. Recently Pastors Tan Seow How (Pastor How) and Lia (Cecilia Chan) wrote a book—*Generations*—about the principles they learned by planting the Heart of God Church and asked me to write an endorsement. I was glad to do it.

## Iceland and a Pharmacy

We had planned the trip to Faroe Island in such a way to make a stop in Iceland on our way back. We flew from Tulsa to England and from there to Denmark and across the ocean to Faroe Island and returned through Reykjavik, Iceland. On our way back, we flew north to Iceland and spent a few days

## A Seminary Dean's Experiment with Servant Leadership

in Reykjavik. It was a short flight from Torshavn to Reykjavík. We could not believe how windy it was when we got off the plane in Reykjavík. As we were leaving the airport and walking toward the taxi we had booked, rolling our baggage, our carry-on bags literally came off the ground due to the power of the wind. It felt like the bags could fly away if we released them. We wondered how the pilots landed the plane in such a windy airport. We do not know if it was normal to have that kind of heavy wind in that city. In any case, it was an unforgettable experience.

Reykjavik was another beautiful place with unique sights and sounds and water everywhere. Due to the climate and the nature of the soil there, Icelanders import almost all their vegetables. It seemed that Iceland was formed out of some mega volcano long ago. Unfortunately, April was a very cold month there and we limited our stay to the main part of the city. We stayed at a beautiful hotel and saw a lot of guests sitting around uniquely made fireplaces and sipping coffee for long periods of time. We found the people in Iceland very friendly and helpful.

While we were in Faroe Island, Molly began to have some symptoms of a cold with an earache and while we were in Iceland, it got worse, and we did not know what to do. Using a map on our iPhone in a foreign language and following the symbol of the pharmacy (Rx), we walked until we found a pharmacy and with the help of the pharmacist who did not understand English very well, we got some over-the-counter medicine and returned to the hotel. The medicine helped just enough to get us back home but without a healing. After we returned through Denmark and London, our son-in-law prescribed an antibiotic which worked, and Molly recovered fully. It seemed like the cold weather and our busy schedule had caused both pneumonia and an ear infection. We were grateful that she did not get so sick that we could not travel back. God helped us to get back home and get the help we needed.

## Jerusalem, Sydney, London, and Kumbanad

I represented the ORU Seminary at three international Empowered21 events and made academic presentations: Israel, Australia, and England. They were all unforgettable experiences, and the one in Australia was especially memorable where I presented a paper at the scholars' meeting held at Alpha Crucis College. It was attended by scholars from different parts of the world, including Dr. Finny Philip from Filadelphia College in North India.

It was an unusual opportunity to get to spend time with Amos Yong, then dean of Regent University Divinity School, and Dr. Vinson Synan, its former dean. We toured the city together, led by the dean of the host College, Jacque Gray. Her book on uniquely Pentecostal interpretations of the Bible had a great impression on me. The cruise on Sydney Harbor in the evening provided by our hosts was also an unforgettable experience. We enjoyed good fellowship, great exchange of ideas, and wonderful sightseeing. I was already impressed with Amos Yong as Dr. Ed Decker and I had spent time with him at an earlier Society for Pentecostal Studies conference. I got to know him better in Australia. I tried to draw him to

ORU before he left for Fuller. He preferred Fuller because of the weather there and due to having close family ties in Los Angeles.

The Empowered21 Conference in Jerusalem was very meaningful as it brought participants from all over the world together in Jerusalem on a Pentecost Sunday. One of the services where Noel Robinson from England led us in worship singing "Rain on me" will stay with all who attended for a long time. One day during the conference I decided to walk back to my hotel to see the area on my way. While passing through a section of the road with no one else around, I looked back and noticed someone following me at a distance. As I walked faster, I saw that person running after me. Scared, I increased my speed. Suddenly, I heard the person following me calling out my name, "Dr. Mathew! Dr. Mathew!" I stopped and turned around to find Fady Zoughbi, an ORU Seminary graduate, now pastoring the House of Bread church in Bethlehem. I was so glad to see his face. He was also attending the conference and had recognized me from a distance as I was leaving the meeting site.

The trip to England was one with special meaning as I was able to spend extra time with two other ORU deans—Dr. Mark Hall and Dr. Ken Weed—and two colleagues from the seminary—Dr. Trevor Grizzle and Dr. Mark Roberts—as we visited particularly important cultural and historical sites in England. Although Molly and I had been to many of the sites during earlier trips to England, especially trips made to preach and teach at Peniel Pentecostal Church and the affiliated Peniel College, this trip was more educational as Dr. Grizzle, a scholar-pastor, had personal history and family in England and Dr. Hall was an expert on C. S. Lewis.

It has been my privilege to preach at various conventions and conferences of the Indian diaspora in North America. I spoke at the largest Asian Pentecostal conference in North America—The Pentecostal Conference of North American Keralites known as PCNAK—annually for many years, from its inception in 1983. I also spoke twice at the largest Pentecostal convention in India known as Kumbanad Convention which is the annual convention of the India Pentecostal Church. I spoke in person in 2012 and on virtual platform in 2021. Dr. Mark Rutland joined me in the 2021 online convention. Dr. Valson Abraham, General President of IPC, who invited us has been a life-long friend and a gracious host. His father Pastor T. S. Abraham and my father K. T. Mathew were ordained in the same service at Kumbanad more than sixty years ago.

## Fellowship of International Students in Tulsa

While being active members in a local church in Tulsa, my family has always been involved in a Bible study and fellowship group of international students from ORU and other Tulsa colleges. There have been several such groups in existence during different times in Tulsa. These groups were held regularly on a weekend night at a nearby church or in the homes of Tulsa residents with international roots. Dr. Tom Luiskutty, a department chairman in the ORU College of Science and Engineering, and I led these groups at different times. Dr. Zach Varghese joined us later and the International

Christian Assembly of Tulsa (ICAT) he now pastors came out of that fellowship.

An influential international student fellowship continues now under the leadership of ORU Seminary graduates Ben and Maggie Chrisostom. This ministry provides practical helps to international students who face unusual challenges and has witnessed several people from non-Christian backgrounds accept Christ as their savior. Many students who sat with us in a circle of study and fellowship in Tulsa have returned to their native lands and now bear witness to Christ in their respective contexts. This group includes seminary graduates Fady Zoughbi in Bethlehem, Israel, and Sharon Joseph in Bangalore, India.

## Seminary's Name Changes

When I was a student at ORU, the theology school was called the School of Theology and Missions (STM). It had a graduate seminary and an undergraduate department of theology. The seminary was then called the Graduate School of Theology and Missions. When Richard Roberts became president, the name was changed to School of Theology and Ministry (STM) with the corresponding name for the graduate seminary. When Dr. Horner became dean, the undergraduate department was made a department of the School of Arts and Sciences. When I became dean in 2000, the undergraduate department was brought back to the School of Theology and Ministry. Initially, the undergraduate faculty had some hesitation about rejoining the seminary, but I met them on several occasions to process their concerns about returning. Eventually, they became an integral part of the STM where I offered them sufficient autonomy. When Dr. Mark Rutland became president, the name of the school changed to College of Theology and Ministry (COTM) having a Department of Theology and a Graduate School of Theology and Ministry (Seminary). A history of the ORU Seminary written by Dr. Larry Hart is available for download from https://digitalshowcase.oru.edu/theo_history/1.

## Hobby Lobby and Mart Green

During a difficult period in the history of ORU, God used David Green, founder of the Hobby Lobby chain of stores, to financially uphold the university. Having had no previous relationship with the university and seeing the threatening financial situation of the institution, Mr. Green felt compassion for the students who would be affected if the university could not survive. He decided to help. His son Mart Green, president of Mardel Christian Stores, was his emissary to the university. The Greens are businesspeople and philanthropists who are well grounded in their family history and Pentecostal faith.

Because of their concern for students preparing for ministry, the Greens had a special interest in the College of Theology and Ministry. Early in their relationship with ORU, I invited Mart Green to attend a faculty meeting in the seminary to address the professors. He joined us in a meeting and reassured us of his family's support and special interest in ministry preparation. I will not forget the stories Mart told us in that meeting about his grandmother and their humble beginnings. She used to make doilies by hand to be sold to church members to raise money for missions, and sometimes wound up buying the products herself when others could not. He said that the Green family could not outgive their grandmother yet. I was able to give Mart a tour of the College and point out the global impact of our graduates. I remain grateful to the Greens for their timely intervention and good will.

## Books, Articles, and Awards

I have been privileged to write books and articles in English and Malayalam languages. I wrote the following books in English: *Ministry Between Miracles, Spirit-led Pastoral Care: Theory and Theology, Spirit-led Ministry in the 21$^{st}$ Century, Spiritual Identity and Spirit-Empowered Life, Leader's Guide for Spiritual Identity and Spirit-Empowered Life, What Will Your Tombstone Say?* and *Ministry Research Simplified.*

I have five books in print in Malayalam: *Yesuvinte Samakalikar* (Contemporaries of Jesus), *Bibilum Manasasthravum* (The Bible and Psychology), *Darsana Malarukal* (A Collection of Published Articles), *Pastoral Care: Theorium Theologium* (Pastoral Care: Theory and Theology), and *Athmaniravinte Susroosha 21-am Noottandil* (Translation of *Spirit-led Ministry in the 21$^{st}$ Century*). *Spirit-led Ministry in the 21$^{st}$ Century* has also been published in the Korean language. An unpublished Spanish translation of this book is used as a textbook in online courses at ORU. *Ministry Between Miracles* has also been translated into the Korean language. In addition to several peer-reviewed journal articles, I have been able to write hundreds of articles in both languages on numerous topics related to Christian life, leadership, and ministry. I have been fortunate to receive several awards from Indian and international writers' forums for two specific books and for general writings. ORU also has recognized my contributions on several occasions with awards for teaching, scholarship, and service.

## Working for Four Presidents and Five Provosts

I had the privilege of working for four presidents—as a chaplain and department head in the City of Faith under the founding president Oral Roberts, and as dean under three others. Everyone's relationship with Oral was special and unique in that we were dealing with the strong personality and authority of the founder. Others functioned like any other college president, except that Richard Roberts was the founder's son and that was a factor in all interactions. As he earned his DMin during my tenure as dean, I had a particularly close relationship with him, and by extension, his wife Lindsay. I also had several opportunities to be involved in ministry with him off campus. A trip to El Salvador to conduct a healing crusade stands out where I saw the Lord using him in a remarkably effective way in a country that was in great distress.

Dr. Mark Rutland was a preacher-president who described his style as "leading from the pulpit" and functioned as a "turn-around president" as described in his book, *Relaunch*. Dr. William M. Wilson, the fourth president I worked for, was a paradigm-shifting leader who came from the ecclesiastical world and led the ORU board prior to his appointment. He appreciated my experience and contributions and involved me in several major projects and sensitive assignments. He was gracious to me personally and professionally and offered me significant benefits during my transition out of deanship which included a yearlong sabbatical, opportunity to return to full-time teaching, and granting me the professor emeritus status. As the longest serving seminary dean at ORU (2000-2016), I have given each president my very best and served them and the university faithfully.

I was fortunate to have exceptionally good personal and professional relationships with all provosts. Dr. Carl Hamilton was the provost when I became Dean Horner's associate. I got to know him better during the transition between Dr. Chappell and Dr. Horner and worked with him during Dr. Horner's tenure. As dean, I had a close relationship with Dr. Ralph Fagin. Fagin was a true servant-leader who had an excellent relationship with all deans and faculty across the campus. He was well liked, respected, and trusted during his time in the provost's office and when he served as interim president. Dr. Mark Lewandowski's time in office was brief but as he was the former dean of the ORU College of Business with whom I had worked, I enjoyed a good relationship with him. Dr. Debbie Sowell was a friend of the seminary and my chapel mate (we sat next to each other in the faculty section in the chapel for many years, and she was my daughter Amy's statistics teacher) and she was sympathetic to my special budget requests on behalf of the School of Theology. Dr. Kathleen Reid-Martinez worked with me as if she found a home in the seminary although her discipline-based academic base was elsewhere.

## Stepping Down from Deanship

I approached President Wilson three times proposing to step down. He wanted me to stay. I approached him a third time after my doctor told me that I must reduce stress in my life. At this point, I shared my desire to step down with provost Dr. Kathleen Reid Martinez and she understood my situation and supported my request. Finally, the president agreed to have me step down as of graduation day 2016 and promised a full year of sabbatical with the plan to return to teach as professor of pastoral care. I was able to write the book *Spiritual Identity and Spirit-Empowered Life* and revise and update the books *Spirit-led Ministry in the 21st Century* and *What Will Your Tombstone Say?* during the sabbatical. Dr. Vinson Synan was named interim dean under whom a search for my replacement could be done. Dr. Synan served as interim dean during my sabbatical year.

A major institutional decision that was made prior to my stepping down from deanship was the hiring of Dr. Wonsuk Ma to lead the PhD program we had been developing. Initially we planned a PhD in Leadership. We also considered a possible PhD in Christian Counseling. Dr. Ed Decker and a hard-working committee served for several years to design the ORU PhD. Dr. Eric Newburgh was a key leader on the PhD committee. He came to ORU with experience with the PhD program at Regent University. Interestingly, I served on a consultation committee while Regent University was developing a PhD program. Dr. Rutland was very supportive as we developed the academic aspects of the PhD program and created projected budgets in consultation with the ATS. With the support and encouragement of Dr. Billy Wilson, I contacted several world class scholars as potential candidates to lead the PhD program. After a long process and many personal contacts with Dr. Wonsuk Ma across the Atlantic where he was the director of the Oxford Centre for Mission Studies in London, we interviewed him and his wife on our campus. Dr. Wonsuk Ma was hired as director of the PhD Program in Global Christianity (now Contextual Theology) and his wife Dr. Julie Ma as a missions professor in the undergraduate department of Theology. The PhD program did commence with Dr. Wonsuk Ma as its director.

Sadly, Dr. Synan fell ill during his interim deanship and Dr. Sam Thorpe who was serving as the undergraduate department chair was appointed to take his place as interim. Later, Dr. Thorpe returned to the chairmanship and Dr. Wonsuk Ma was appointed to serve as the sixth dean of the College of Theology and Ministry.

## Back to Professorship, Retirement, and New Mission

During the sabbatical, Molly and I had been praying about investing our life in leadership development within the growing Pentecostal movement in India. Based on our experience in theological higher education, we felt that the best way to do this would be to help train Pentecostal/charismatic ministers in India who could not afford to go abroad for higher studies at the highest professional level through accredited indigenous Doctor of Ministry programs.

I have been working with Dr. John Thannickal and his son Steve Thannickal of New Life College, Bangalore and Dr. Valson Abraham of India Bible College and Seminary in Kerala about starting Doctor of Ministry programs in their institutions. These would be world class doctoral programs that would be indigenous, conforming to local economic situations, and accredited by the Asia Theological Association (ATA). The Thannickal and Abraham families have been trusted friends of both our families for generations. At India Bible College and Seminary, this would be the first fully indigenous accredited Pentecostal DMin in "God's own country." This school is related to the India Pentecostal Church (IPC), the largest indigenous Pentecostal denomination in India, in which both Molly's and my parents and grandparents had served sacrificially.

I was also invited by Dr. Eim to help to establish a DMin program at a new Pentecostal theological seminary in Korea. This request appealed to us because it was also addressing a need in Asia and was connected to another trusted brother in the Lord.

I returned from the sabbatical to teach full-time in fall 2017 while Dr. Sam Thorpe was interim dean, but felt it was time to leave the professorship by May 2018 to pursue the new challenge God was placing before us. Dr. Sam Thorpe initiated a plan to grant me dean emeritus status but as there was no provision for that in the ORU faculty handbook, a proposal was made to recommend emeritus status as professor.

# A Seminary Dean's Experiment with Servant Leadership

My announcement to step down from deanship in 2016 was a big surprise to the COTM, especially to the seminary faculty and staff. One staff member wrote a poem expressing her sense of loss due to my transition and presented it to me. Only Judy Cope, my administrative assistant, and Dr. Cheryl Iverson, associate dean, had been given a heads up, so students and faculty were surprised. Leaving so soon from teaching in May 2018 was also not expected. I was given several formal and informal farewells when I left the deanship and when I left the teaching post.

Molly also retired from St. Francis Hospital after serving as a registered nurse for thirty years. People at the hospital grieved over her leaving but wished us well as they knew that we were embarking on God's new mission for our lives. We have been fortunate to travel extensively and lay the foundations for the DMin degrees at all three institutions before the Covid-19 pandemic prohibited international travels. All three programs have been formally initiated and because travel is still limited, we are thankful to be able to teach the students and coach the faculty now with the help of modern technology.

Working with the faculty and students in the doctoral programs at these schools is what we are involved in now. Training ministers at the highest academic and professional levels in Asia is our new mission. As we feel led, we are fully volunteer missionaries in this effort.

*Part II*

## Stories

*Chapter 5*

# Stories from India

## A Snake in My Path

My earliest memories include my mother working as a schoolteacher and my father as a pastor. By the time I was 10 years old, he was pastoring a church in a village called Vechoochira near the eastern hilly area of Kerala, filled with lush forests and noisy creeks, with newly created narrow mud roads, thatched-roof houses, and a lot of poisonous snakes. We walked everywhere in those days. Walking a mile or two to school was not unusual. Only Jeeps could handle the muddy roads winding up the steep hills. Bullock carts and lorries carried rubber sheets and other cargo to markets away from town. A noisy open market was at the center of town, and it was the most popular meeting place. Private buses made roundtrips from Vechoochira to two or three cities twenty or thirty miles away. Deaths by snakebites was common in our community where most people developed a phobia regarding snakes. No wonder I never got used to the American idea of having a pet snake!

One day I was on my way to school, walking along a narrow path that ran through the middle of our hillside community. I noticed something moving and was shocked to see a snake across my path with its moving tail clearly visible. I stood frozen but screamed at the top of my voice, shouting that there was a snake in my path and asking someone to come running to help me. People came out of their houses and one man ran toward me carrying a long stick. I stood right where I was as he approached the snake carefully. I waited for him to hit the snake, but he just stood there looking toward the head of the snake which I could not see. He then started to laugh. I got upset and asked him why he was not hitting the snake. He asked me if I had seen the head of the snake. I said, "No." He asked me to take a look. I tried to peek and found the head of the snake looking flat and unmoving, with the tail still moving.

I guessed what happened. Someone had gone before me, found the snake, and hit it on the head. The snake was as good as dead, but its life had not gone out completely, so the tail was moving. My neighbor carried the snake on his stick and walked off and I went on my way.

As the serpent represents Satan in Christian theology, I have used this encounter with the snake in my sermons to illustrate that Jesus has gone before us and bruised the head of the serpent as prophesied in Genesis (Gen 3:15). The serpent can try to frighten us but cannot harm us fatally. A poisonous snake does not kill with its tail! We do not need to be afraid of the old snake for he is a defeated foe, and we are well aware of his devices (2 Cor 2:11).

## Two Blind People

Two blind people had a great impact on my life. One was a former Brahmin young lady who spoke at our church when I was a boy. She was from Andhra Pradesh and spoke Telugu language. As my father knew that language as a result of serving in Andhra Pradesh with his uncle Pastor G. Samuel, he translated her message into Malayalam, the local language. This young woman was the only daughter in a prestigious Brahmin family. She wanted to learn English and her parents hired a Christian teacher who used the English Bible as a textbook. As a result of reading the Bible and studying it, this young lady accepted Christ as her savior but kept it a secret because she feared her family would discover her decision and would not accept it. Once it was discovered, her brother demanded that she give up her new-found faith, but she refused. He gave her an ultimatum, stating that if she would not give up her faith in Jesus, he would pluck her eyes out. She held on to her faith and her brother fulfilled his threat, and we were listening to a beautiful young woman who was blind.

I do not remember if I heard her story before I made my public confession of faith in Christ or after, but her story has stayed with me throughout my life. I remember her saying that she would see again and that the first face she would see would be the face of her savior Jesus Christ. [I thank God for my devout Hindu classmates from BMC who have never shown an ounce of disrespect or hate for my Christian faith or Pentecostal background! They have been very kind and receptive to my input on issues of importance from a Christian perspective.]

The second blind person who had an impact on my life was an evangelist named Markos. A man who lost his clear vision, Evangelist Markos could only see things like shadows. He walked using a cane and traveled extensively, preaching and conducting revival meetings. He was a regular visitor to our family as my father was very fond of him. He conducted several old-time tarrying meetings in our church. Pentecostal churches used to conduct tarrying meetings to help members receive the baptism of the Holy Spirit. He was always welcome in our house and his ministry was received well by the church.

In a tarrying meeting he led at our church in 1961, just a few months after my new birth experience, I was filled with the Holy Spirit. I remember the evangelist laying hands on me and praying for me. I also remember one of my cousins staying with me and continuing to pray. That experience, although it happened at a young age, was truly a defining moment in my life. Evangelist Markos has had such an impact on my entire family that both my brother John, who as a young person had several opportunities to help him to get around, and I have written about our regard for this humble servant of Jesus Christ.

## Nervous Kid, Future Preacher

As a youngster, I suffered from an awfully bad case of stage-fright. I remember one occasion when I was to give a speech in my sixth-grade class at St. Thomas School. My mother helped me to prepare a good speech. I memorized the speech and looked forward to delivering it to impress my classmates. I kept the speech written in pencil in my shirt pocket, opening it and reading it several times during the day, waiting for the last class period when the meeting was to be held. As the meeting started, I began to feel nervous and by the time I was called to give my speech, I could hardly stand up. I made my way to the front of the class, unfolded the paper, and started to read. My hands began to shake but I kept reading; however, the shaking got worse until I tore up the paper before I could finish the speech. Everyone laughed. I felt so humiliated and thought I was going to pass out. I was so relieved that it was the last class period of the day. I went home and told the story to my mother. She comforted me and told me not to give up but to try again next time. Reluctantly I signed up again and am glad that I did, as I had no clue at that time that some decades later, I would be making public presentations in a second language to diverse audiences in multiple nations. I still get nervous when I have to make a public presentation, especially before a large or unfamiliar audience, but I am able to manage it much better than when I was in the sixth grade.

## Missing Mrs. Gandhi

I was a commuter or "day scholar" at Mar Thoma College. It was announced one day in class that Indian Prime Minister Mrs. Indira Gandhi was coming through town and classes would be cancelled to allow students to see the prime minister. The entire student body left campus and walked a mile to line up along Main Central Road in Thiruvalla. Students from nearby institutions and the public lined up on both sides of the wide road. The crowd held people of all faiths, and a host of students and teachers. It was a hot and sunny day, and the people were pressing against each other where I was standing. All the public bus services were cancelled for the afternoon. I stood there with my books in my hands, feeling hot and tired. Suddenly, I realized that I was passing out and falling. All was black for a moment.

When I woke up and opened my eyes, I was on a table at a roadside tea shop. I did not know how much time had passed. A man who appeared to be a farmer stood by me holding my books. He bought me a cup of hot coffee, or maybe tea. I sat up and drank the beverage. I felt the heat and comfort of that drink as I stared at the man. As I became more conscious and alert, he handed my books to me and asked me if I had money for bus fare. I checked my pockets and said I did. When he saw that I was okay, he began to walk away. I asked him who he was. He smiled and just said, "I am a Christian." I never got to see Mrs. Gandhi as she had already passed by, and I got home safely by taking the next available bus to Niranam.

I never knew who that man was who also must have missed Mrs. Gandhi. I used to think that he was an angel. He could have been an angel as they are our ministering spirits according to the epistle to the Hebrews, but it is very possible that he was an Indian Christian farmer, a person who was representing the kingdom of God, who walked away from the crowd that included all sorts of people, and the chance to see Mrs. Gandhi, to help me, a person in need.

In that sense, the kingdom of God came my way on that hot South Indian day in the shoes of an Indian farmer. If I were not a Christian that day, imagine the potential impact of his words, "I am a Christian," on me. This thought has remained with me all my life and I have told many groups of students the importance of representing the kingdom of God in the very ordinary things in their lives. May God help us to be engaged in the business of the kingdom of God that may not look religious but will have a great impact on the world. In so doing we would become God's true messengers.

## When Character is Lost

It was a custom in colleges in Kerala to have friends and teachers sign an autograph, a small booklet with colorful papers where they could write memories or wishes and sign their names, during the last few days of the final semester of studies. Some people inscribe funny quotes, others may recall experiences or write down best wishes. This was an especially meaningful exercise at Bishop Moore College where our class was a small one and we spent most of the three years together in the same classroom. Some of my classmates who had completed the pre-degree and degree programs at Bishop Moore had spent five years together. Something one classmate, Lalithambal C., a shy female student from a very conservative Hindu family, wrote in my autograph had an impact on my life. She wrote:

When wealth is lost, nothing is lost.

When health is lost, something is lost.

When character is lost, everything is lost!

I do not know her source, but her words had a lasting influence. I shared these words with my daughters when they were teenagers.

After reconnecting with some of my classmates online, Molly and I had the opportunity to meet two of them—Col. Hari and Rema—in Bangalore during a trip to India. Rema had traveled from Kerala to Bangalore just to meet us. She called Lalithambal during our meeting and gave me a chance to speak to our classmate, whom I had not seen nor spoken to since our last day in college more than four decades earlier. She told me on the phone that she had been ill for a while and expressed the hope of meeting us in person during our next trip to India. I told her that I had memorized her words in the autograph and how they had an influence on my life. Not long after, I received word that our dear classmate passed away. Although she is gone, her simple words remain with me.

## My Father's Shoe Repairman

All immigrants with family members left behind in their old countries must deal with getting untimely phone calls regarding the death of a loved one. One is never prepared to receive such calls no matter how expected they might be, especially if the news is regarding a beloved parent. Molly and I have received such calls when we least expected them. One of the most difficult trips I have made to India was in response to such a call regarding my father.

The funeral brought together friends and family from all over Kerala and beyond, along with many of my father's current and former coworkers in ministry. Although it was a painful pilgrimage, the trip gave us much comfort as we were able to celebrate his life as a faithful servant of God. At the funeral service, I spoke about our family's self-understanding by making reference to the conversation between Joseph's brothers and the Pharaoh of Egypt as recorded in Genesis:

> "Pharaoh asked the brothers, 'What is your occupation?' 'Your servants are shepherds,' they replied to Pharaoh, 'just as our fathers were,'" (Gen. 47:3).

Recognizing that I had a legacy of shepherding gave me much comfort.

At the end of the service, one of the pastors from the area where my father was District Pastor for thirty years approached me and expressed special appreciation for his impact on his life. I asked him to give me some details. He said, "When I met your father for the first time, I met him as his shoe repairman. Today I am a minister of the gospel because he discipled me and mentored me." I was moved by his testimony, especially as I realized that my father did not have the privilege of receiving theological higher education at well-known institutions, but he had the knowledge, skills, and grace to turn his shoe repairman into a fulltime pastor! I wish I had what he had. He remains my ministry hero.

*Chapter 6*

# Stories from Yale and New Haven

## Lunch with Osami

Osami Sadaie was a Methodist pastor from Kyoto, Japan who enrolled in the STM program at Yale Divinity School. Both of us arrived on campus at the same time and were neighbors in the Bushnell dormitory. Osami was more homesick than I was as he had left behind a wife and young kids in Japan. I saw him tear up at times when he mentioned them. Although Yale dining rooms probably had the best rotating campus menus in the nation, which included regular international dinner nights, Osami and I missed our native foods in the first weeks of our life on campus.

On a Saturday, Osami decided to have something different to eat for lunch. He went downtown and bought some canned foods. Bushnell had no kitchen facilities and the only appliance he had was a coffee maker, which was actually a water boiler to make tea or coffee. Osami asked me to skip the refectory and join him in his room for lunch. I joined him as a couple of cans were getting heated in his small water boiler. When they were sufficiently heated, Osami took a manual can opener and started to open a can. I was not familiar with the brand of food but as he opened the can, I told him that the food did not smell very good. He ignored me and took a spoon to taste the food, but as he turned, I saw the words on the can and read out loud, "Nine Lives," cat food! We broke out in laughter and rushed to the refectory before it closed.

Osami graduated and returned to Japan where he served as a beloved Christian pastor in the Buddhist nation. We kept writing to each other for several years, often recalling our life in Bushnell.

## Man in His Sunday Suit!

During my YDS days, I used to take the Trailways bus from New Haven and go down to New York City to visit my relative John Varghese. I used to leave on Saturday mornings and return on Sunday afternoons after attending worship at one of the pioneering churches of Indian immigrants. On a very normal Sunday morning, we were on our way to church and waiting on the subway platform for the train to arrive. There was a very well-dressed man standing not far from us. We noticed nothing unusual about the man as he looked like someone dressed for church, 1970s style. The train approached the station and to our utter shock we saw the man jump in front of it, looking as if he'd been glued to the indenting windshield as the train moved forward.

We witnessed a suicide. Train services were cancelled temporarily, and we were so traumatized that we decided to return to the apartment. We could hardly move but walked back slowly and tried to talk about what we had just witnessed but found that conversation too difficult. I have never been able to forget that man as he still reminds me that we can never go by looks when it comes to people's pains and must use every opportunity to respectfully share Christian hope and the good news of Jesus Christ with anyone and everyone and at every opportunity. I have wondered many times what that day might have been like if I had introduced myself and engaged in a conversation with that unknown man in his fine Sunday suit.

## One of a Kind Driver's License Test

My first appearance for a driver's license exam in New Haven, Connecticut remains unforgettable. As an international student on scholarship, I did not own a car at that time and paid an extra fee to use the driving school's car for my road test. My driving instructor picked me up on campus and took me to the motor vehicle department at the scheduled time. I passed the written test, went through the eye exam, and my instructor lined up the car at the appropriate starting point for the road test. I got in the car and waited.

When the turn came to demonstrate my skills, the inspecting officer got inside the car and sat in the passenger seat. Following his instructions, I started the car, went through the initial preparations, and began to drive. I had chosen a car with manual shift for my training as most cars in India did not have automatic transmission in those days and I was planning to return to India after my education. As I drove, suddenly I became very nervous and anxious, my left leg began to shake, and I could not keep my left foot on the clutch. I tried to hide my anxiety and continued to drive, turning left and right as instructed.

As I continued to drive, the shaking of my left leg increased. We came on a hill, and I was not able to keep the car moving forward and at one point it began to roll back. I used all the skills I had and got it to move forward again, but with a very strong jerk. The inspector told me to move the car to the side of the road and stop. I did. He asked me to get out of my seat and take the passenger seat. I did. Without saying another word, he took the driver's seat, made a U-turn, and drove back to the motor vehicles department. When I got out of the passenger seat at the end of the longest road trip I have ever taken, the inspector told me to take more lessons and not to come back for a license for at least 30 days. I thanked him, and the driving instructor, who looked really depressed, gave me a ride back to campus. I was so humiliated and was convinced that I would never get a license.

I took more lessons, this time on a car with automatic transmission, giving up my ambition to get licensed using a manual shift. After completing several additional lessons at a cost exceeding my student budget and running Mr. Kaiser's blue Volkswagen into the ditch a couple of times, I took the driver's license test again and finally received my license. I was excited, but I would never forget the sadness and shame I felt when I failed the first time. As I have not failed any school tests in my life, it was a hard and needed lesson for me to learn how it feels to fail in something that everybody else seems to pass easily.

## Dial and Raid

My first summer job was at a department store called Daniels in Wallingford, Connecticut. Although I had a bike by then, it was too hard to ride to work because of the hilly areas surrounding the Kaisers' beautiful custom-made residence where I stayed during summer months. The Kaisers gave me a ride to and from work every day. I did not have a TV in my dormitory room during the first year or the time to watch enough commercials to be familiar with the brand names of consumer products in this country. This made being a salesperson on the floor of the department store challenging. I had multiple duties at Daniel's, including moving products, stocking, and helping customers. I was a good worker except that I had trouble finding certain products customers asked for, especially those known only by brand names (Crest vs. toothpaste).

One day a lady came and started looking for some product. Not being able to find it she approached me and asked to help her. I asked her the name of the product she was looking for. She told me that she wanted Dial. I did not know what Dial was. I only knew that watches had dials. I asked her to describe the product to me. She described a spray can with a particular color, and I took off to look for the product.

I was happy to find a can fitting the description and brought it back to her, but I was shocked when she started swearing at me and being really angry.

No wonder, I had given her a can of Raid, a roach killer, instead of a deodorant. The lady was so upset and went to the manager to report her displeasure. The manager apologized to the woman for me. I have told this story in many places to demonstrate how difficult it is to communicate cross-culturally and how difficult it is to be an immigrant in a very unfamiliar culture, especially without many of the resources. Thankfully, I was not fired that day and was able to work until the end of the summer and return to campus.

## Give Your Five Loaves

I will never forget the words Dean Colin Williams of Yale Divinity School delivered on the day I graduated with the MDiv degree. Mr. Williams (no one at Yale is called Dr.) was a biblical scholar from Australia and a great theological educator. He told us to celebrate our accomplishment of graduating from YDS, but to remember that our degrees and all our knowledge, skills, and talents together added up to only five loaves of bread. He told us that we would be facing a multitude soon and five loaves would never feed a multitude. So, he exhorted us to give our five loaves to Jesus who would bless them, break them, and multiply them to feed the multitude. He promised us that if we followed his instruction, we would never lack anything as there would be plenty left over after the multitude is fed. I have never been able to get the picture of Jesus blessing the five loaves of my life out of my mind. It remains a lifelong reminder of my inadequacies to fulfill God's purposes with my skills alone and of my utter need to depend on God. I have shared Dean Williams' words with many graduating classes at Oral Roberts University.

## Panic Area

I recall the first time I drove to Norwich Hospital during the winter in the first car I owned, a used 1969 Plymouth Barracuda I had bought from a member of Gospel Tabernacle, Grace Barrett. When I left the Kaiser's house in Wallingford after spending a weekend there, the sun was shining, and it looked like a typical New England fall day. Soon after I started, it began to snow and before long the snow turned to ice. I had no experience driving in the snow or ice and became fearful as the car began to skid. I slowed down and tried to move forward as slowly as I could. I was at a place with no markers to give me an idea regarding my location. This was before space satellites and GPS and all the apps we now have in our iPhones to give us geographic orientation.

I began to panic as I put my break on and had no response. The car began to slide to the side of the highway and finally stopped. I was surprised to see no other cars nearby. Apparently, everyone else knew a blizzard was on its way. I strained my eyes looking for any sign to identify my location and was pleased to notice a blue and white sign, but my fear increased as I read the words on it, "panic area!" I could not believe what I was seeing. I had never seen a sign saying, "panic area." It took me a few moments to realize that in my distress I was misreading the sign which actually said, "picnic area." I have used this story in many places to illustrate how being in a panic mode does not help in crisis situations and how we see things in a worse way as we look at them without faith.

## Free Breakfast and Eternal Life

I met Richard Everett at a Full Gospel Business Men's Fellowship (FGBMF) breakfast meeting in New Haven where I was invited to speak. He was a young man who was invited by a friend to attend the breakfast meeting. In his own words, "I went for the free food." I shared my testimony and presented the gospel and Richard responded to the message and accepted Christ. Later he and his wife Mary Sue became a part of our church in New Haven, and he was an active member and a great young leader. Richard was a gifted businessman. As God blessed him financially, he was a blessing to the church. Despite several financial setbacks, God really blessed him through the years.

I lost touch with Richard after I left the church. Some years ago, I heard from him about a book he wrote on Christian stewardship, titled *Whatever Happened to the Promised Land?* The manuscript described how through Christian stewardship which included faithful tithing he paid off $250,000 debt and eventually became a successful businessman and a credentialed financial advisor. The book stated that he owned a financial advising firm that managed considerable assets. I wrote an endorsement for the book. In the published version of the book, he mentioned how he has been "heaven-bound" ever since he heard the gospel from me for the first time at a restaurant.

I heard recently from my nephew, Solomon Thimothy, that he ran into Richard Everett, whom he did not know, in a business situation. Quite unexpectedly, he spoke to my nephew about our first encounter at the breakfast decades ago. Although I have not seen him in years, I was pleased to hear that Richard is still involved in business and bearing witness to the life-transforming power of the good news of Jesus Christ.

## From Alcohol to Street Ministry

One of the individuals I met at Gospel Tabernacle was a young man, Dick Delocco. I met Dick first as the husband of a church member. One day he came in through the main door of the church during a worship service, yelling and saying, "You have brainwashed my wife." He was fully drunk. After meeting with him at the end of the service in my office where the deacons had kept him, I learned that he was the husband of a recent follower of Jesus who attended our church. He was suffering from addiction to alcohol. He told us how he had been arrested in the past for breaking into a gas station to steal money to buy alcohol. He said that his wife had drastically changed after coming to our church and that she was acting like a holy woman! I tried to explain to Dick that his wife had accepted Christ as her savior who changed her life for the better and that we did not brainwash her. We invited him to accept Christ who would change his life for the better. He did not respond to the invitation then but left calmer.

I do not recall the exact day when he accepted Christ, but Dick Delocco became a follower of Jesus and a very committed member of Gospel Tabernacle. After God healed him from alcoholism, Dick began to respond to everyone asking, "How are you?" with one word — "Fantastic!" Eventually, whenever we met, we greeted each other with the word, "Fantastic!" Dick became a fantastic brother to me. I still remember his joyful face as he pronounced in his special style, "Fan-tastic!"

Many years after I left New Haven, I learned that Dick Delocco was ministering among the homeless and people struggling with alcoholism in the downtown area of New Haven. Recently I came across his obituary online, quite accidentally, which mentioned his street ministry in New Haven.

## Chronic Pain and Service to God

Frank Battista was a member of Gospel Tabernacle. He used to be an active member of the nearby Catholic Church. He was a bank employee who had an accident at his workplace sometime before we met him. He slipped and fell and experienced significant damage to his body, forcing him to leave employment. He felt depressed about his situation and suffered much. His doctor encouraged him to engage in some meaningful volunteer work to overcome the depression. So, he devoted his life to visiting the sick as a volunteer at Yale New Haven Hospital on a regular basis. He would go early in the morning each day and help people with anything he could do for them, just trying to cheer them up, which began to heal his own emotions. Many well-known people received Frank's unselfish service, and some wanted to reward him with gifts, but he refused all gifts.

Battista and his wife accepted Christ and I was privileged to baptize them. They became active members of the congregation and became key persons during the building project which was yet to come. They were involved in various aspects of the church and its ministry and sang regularly in the church choir. Frank told the story of his own healing through volunteer work and prayer in many public gatherings. When a new church was built in North Haven, Battista asked his former benefactors to send any gift they had wished to give him to the building fund. We received numerous donations in his honor.

## Serving God When One Cannot Read

There was a new follower of Jesus who made a great impression on my life. His life was transformed by an encounter with Jesus. He wanted to serve the Lord in a meaningful way. However, this good brother was not fortunate enough to get the education to be a fully literate person. But that did not stop him from serving the Lord faithfully in the church. He could not lead groups or teach Sunday school classes, but he had a valid driver's license and a good driving record. He dedicated himself to using his driver's license to help people attend Sunday school and worship services. He picked up children and young people from low-income housing areas and other neighborhoods and brought them to church functions. Because of his dedication, many came who could not otherwise attend due to lack of transportation. It was beautiful to see him using his gifts and talents to serve the Lord despite the literacy challenge he had. He did become an adult learner and remains a hero to me.

## Baptizing a Senior Saint

Mrs. Mary Bloomfield was a resident of the Masonic Home, a convalescent home, in Wallingford when I was a field education student during my MDiv studies. Through our interactions, she accepted Christ and became a friend to me, an international student then. Later, after I became the pastor of Gospel Tabernacle, one of Mrs. Broomfield's caregivers, Violet, who had also become a believer in Christ in the meantime, used to bring her to church occasionally. One day there was a baptismal service at the church and Mrs. Bloomfield expressed her desire to be baptized. I had mixed feelings about baptizing an older saint her age, but yielded to her request and spent time with her to prepare her for baptism.

Violet brought Mrs. Bloomfield to the church to be baptized. I baptized several people in the baptistry, which was in the sanctuary right in front of the pulpit. When her turn came, Mrs. Broomfield was brought before me in the water by her caregiver and others who helped. I immersed her in water after she confessed her faith but as I raised her out of the water, we were all in shock to see her choking. She had opened her mouth underwater and swallowed some water and was struggling to breathe. I was really shaking and momentarily thought of how awful it would be if something bad happened to this old saint.

My friend and a lay leader at the church, Sal Rivera, was a policeman in New Haven at that time. He was one of the people helping candidates get in and out of the baptistry. Seeing Mrs. Bloomfield in distress, he rushed down the steps

# A Seminary Dean's Experiment with Servant Leadership

of the baptistry, picked her up with his hands, and pushed her belly with his knee in the Heimlich fashion to get the water out of her. A lot of water seemed to come out of her mouth. We all took a collective sigh of relief as she began to breathe normally, saying "Praise the Lord."

Sal Rivera has remained a close friend for decades. My parents, who met him during their visit to New Haven in 1980, loved him like a son. He visited us in Tulsa when my father came back to visit us. My mother passed away in 1996, and Sal maintained a relationship with my father until his homegoing in 2002.

## Now You Have a Building Fund

You may recall how Mrs. Edna Livingston gave me two one-dollar bills as I left Gospel Tabernacle church in New Haven after my first visit there from Yale Divinity School. I became pastor of the church in 1976 and in just two years, somehow by the grace of God, this New England church grew enough that all the available seats in the main sanctuary were being used during Sunday services. Seating in the sanctuary and parking on the streets became major problems. Buying some nearby land to create a new parking lot and updating the building, or a possible move out of the current location became a matter of discussion. As a pastor just out of the divinity school, I was still learning to take care of the spiritual needs of the congregation and was not in a position to start a building project. But one day when Molly and I visited Mrs. Livingston, the need of a new church building came up in our conversation. As we left her, she gave me an envelope with a check for $1,000 in it. I asked her what that money was for. She said it was for the building fund. I told her that we did not have a building fund yet. She smiled and said, "Now you have a building fund." That was the beginning of a building fund for the new church complex in North Haven, Connecticut.

## Emotion, Devotion, and Commotion

Charlie was a faithful member of Gospel Tabernacle. A man who appeared to be in his thirties, he was involved in men's fellowship and other evangelistic ministries in the church. He was a single person who did not seem to be interested in getting married. I was surprised one day to see Charlie sitting in his usual pew but next to a beautiful young woman. They seemed like a good couple. The young lady attended the church for several weeks after that day and he seemed to enjoy her company, sometimes to the point of distraction from the service.

I noticed one Sunday that they were sitting away from each other at two different ends of the sanctuary. As he left the service, I asked Charlie what was happening between them. I fully understood his answer: "Pastor Mathew! A lot of emotion without any devotion is a lot of commotion!"

## Two Priests and a Pentecostal

There was a Catholic church across the street from Gospel Tabernacle, not far from it. Through the testimony of Frank Battista, several others who had been members of this church visited our services. Initially they were just visitors and eventually many of them left the Catholic church and became members of our church. As a young pastor, I was happy to see the Catholic visitors becoming members of our church. I had a sense of pride in what I saw happening. My pride collapsed one day as I received a cash gift for the building of our new sanctuary from the Catholic priest who was losing church members. The Holy Spirit showed me that the priest was a better disciple of Jesus Christ than I was. This was a meaningful experience in my life as an Indian Pentecostal and it had a lasting impact on my approach to Catholic friends and their church. God used this priest to give me a better Christian attitude about my Catholic brothers and sisters.

Another Catholic priest played a role in my attitude adjustment. Father Francis was a Keralite doctoral student in Catholic theology at the Vatican in Italy and was temporarily assisting the nearby Catholic parish. He was staying with the local priest and watched a local television news program reporting on the growth of our church, featuring a Sunday service and pointing out that the pastor was a YDS graduate from Kerala. Father Francis made it a point to visit us and introduce himself. He was such a wonderful person that we invited him to stay with us at the parsonage. We spent much time discussing Kerala and Christian theology. He was a loving clergyman and impressed us with his love of God and concern for humanity. We took pictures of him carrying our baby daughter Amy. After that visit he stayed in touch with us for few years but lost contact three decades ago.

Our relationship with Father Francis had a significant impact on Molly and me and it had a special impact on me in terms of changing my unwholesome attitude toward the Catholic church and clergy. After more than three decades of having no contacts, in 2019, we received a phone call from Father Francis who was in New Zealand. He got our new phone number somehow and called to check on our safety during a predicted hurricane. We learned that he has recently retired and is living in New Zealand. He had spent several years in ministry in Kerala and had just completed a pastoral assignment in New Zealand.

*Chapter 7*

# Stories from City of Faith

## Visiting Patients with Oral Roberts

Visiting hospital patients with Oral Robert was a special experience. I had the opportunity to accompany him on many such visits as I had done with both Richard and Lindsay Roberts. It was really a privilege.

Most of the patients, especially those from out of state or other countries, came because of Oral Roberts. They were his "partners" and had great faith in his ministry. A lot of them were regular contributors to the ministry. Some would have traded their doctors for Oral Roberts. Oral did not make surprise visits. His office gave us enough warning to prepare for the visits. Normally they took place in the afternoons. Sometimes he was responding to a specific request from a patient. Other times we could choose the patients he visited.

In any case, I made sure that I had visited each patient before he did to make sure that we had an idea of the patients' particular situations on the given day. We did not want to run into an unpleasant situation with Oral or the patients. There were occasions when a patient who was too sick to lift his hand to shake my hand during my visit in the morning would jump out of his bed to shake Oral's hand. In some cases, patients who were prayed for by Oral Roberts were discharged sooner than expected. I used to wonder about this phenomenon: Was it because of their faith in him? Was it because he was a celebrity? Or was it simply the grace of God working in and through him?

I was convinced that there was a special call on this man and that the grace of God manifested in his ministry in a powerful way to minister healing to many. One thing I noticed was that as Oral Roberts entered a hospital room to pray, there appeared to be a change in his countenance that reflected a deep compassion as if the patient was his own flesh and blood. That was not a show. Oral Roberts felt something deep within him that caused him to connect with hurting people. I wonder if that compassion itself was his special grace.

It has been my privilege to study Oral Roberts' theology of healing and had it published in the peer reviewed journal of Theology *Spiritus* titled, "Oral Roberts' Theology of Healing: A Journey from Pentecostal 'Divine Healing' to Charismatic 'Signs and Wonders' to Spirit-empowered 'Whole Person Healing.'" This article can be downloaded freely at: https://digitalshowcase.oru.edu/spiritus/vol3/iss2/13

## Undeserved Credit for Healing

A significant event took place at the City of Faith that was shared with the partners of the Oral Roberts Ministry. Lindsay, Oral's daughter-in-law, was admitted to the City of Faith as a surgery patient. People of faith around the country prayed for her, and I visited her as a prayer partner as she was in my assigned area of responsibility. On the day of the surgery, her husband Richard Roberts (before he was President and Dr.) was with her as I visited them. Before she was taken to the surgical suits, Richard and I joined in a prayer for her.

I kept an eye open to see her returning after surgery but was surprised to see her come back just a short time after leaving the room. I was told that she did not need the surgery as the doctors could not find the tumor that was supposed to be removed. I heard Lindsay's public testimony later where she stated that if that surgery had been done, she would not be the proud mother of three daughters today!

There is no way to know whose prayer was answered by God. Certainly, prayer of faith by everyone was honored, but somehow, within the hospital unit, I was associated with Lindsay's healing as I was the last person praying with the family before she left for surgery. I received some added attention for a short while but knew without any doubt that the credit only belonged to God and all His people who interceded for Lindsay.

## Oral in the Audience

Oral Roberts University requires all students, faculty, and staff to attend two chapel services per week. Everything shuts down on campus during chapel hours normally; however, due to their assignments and clinical work in the City of Faith Hospital, it became very difficult for many doctors and medical students to attend chapel services in the main chapel building. So, chapel services for medical faculty and students were held in the auditorium on the 60$^{th}$ floor of the City of Faith building. Staff prayer partners took turns preaching at these services while the campus-wide services where being held at the main chapel.

It was my turn to preach one day in the City of Faith chapel service. I took a passage from the Gospel of John Chapter 6 and began to prepare my message. I noticed that the chapter began with the feeding of the 5,000 and ended with Jesus asking his disciples if they would also want to leave him as the people who ate the bread had.

In reading through the remaining chapters of John, a question came up in my mind that was very relevant for everyone working at the City of Faith at that time. People were coming from all over the United States and several other nations to be treated at the City of Faith after hearing about the merging of medicine and prayer and especially after seeing Oral Roberts' television programs talking about the miracles that were taking place in his ministry. Many of the programs featured videos of healings from his evangelistic ministry and the current work of whole person health care at the City of Faith.

Oral Roberts was the first television evangelist in the world as he brought many scenes of healing from his tent crusades into the living rooms of America. Millions of people followed his ministry and became partners with him in the

## A Seminary Dean's Experiment with Servant Leadership

various projects he had and particularly in the building of the City of Faith. Although we did not have a sufficient number of inpatients to meet the budgetary needs of the facility due to multiple reasons, many patients did come expecting miracles even though they were being treated in a science-based medical practice with the intentionally added benefits of faith and prayer. There were many patients who were disappointed that they did not receive a supernatural miracle while they were at the City of Faith Hospital.

This was also a time when the word of faith division of the charismatic movement was prominent, emphasizing faith alone for healing. Rhema Bible College in Broken Arrow founded by evangelists Kenneth Hagin was the leading proponent of this theology at that time. As we encountered more and more disappointed patients, despite many testimonies of healing through natural and supernatural means taking place at the City of Faith, there were many discussions among the staff about the question of supernatural miracles taking place in a medical complex.

In this context, as I was reading the chapters in the gospel of John to prepare a sermon, this question formed in my mind: What really happened between miracles in Jesus' life and ministry? I was able to discern from the Gospel of John certain things that Jesus did between the miracles. My observations from John's gospel became my sermon in the City of Faith chapel service which was attended by medical school faculty and students working in the clinic and hospital.

It so happened that on the day I preached that message, the dean of the School of Theology and Missions, Dr. Jimmy

Buskirk, attended the City of Faith chapel service. The message was well received by those in attendance and at the end of the service Dr. Buskirk approached me and asked me to preach the same message at the forthcoming monthly university faculty chapel. I was excited about the opportunity and somewhat apprehensive about preaching to a large group of PhDs, not knowing exactly how this message would be received. I did not have a doctorate at that time which made it psychologically more difficult to address this distinguished group.

The time came for me to attend the faculty chapel. The teaching auditorium (Room 4114 on the fourth floor of the Graduate Center) was filled with faculty and administration. Suddenly, I noticed President Oral Roberts walking into the auditorium. I was not expecting him to attend faculty chapel and became extremely concerned, worrying that I would offend him or contradict his teaching in some way and would be in big trouble. As I began to present my message, I noticed Oral Roberts paging through his Bible and my concern increased. I preached and sat down, glad that the message was over and that Oral Roberts was still there. I was extremely relieved when I received his approval of my presentation before he left the auditorium.

I had no idea at that time that that message would become the foundation for a theology of pastoral care from a Pentecostal/charismatic perspective. Years later, I was able to develop that concept into a book with the title *Ministry Between Miracles,* which was first published in 2002. This book has had an impact on my students and the churches they pastor, and in places where I taught pastoral care as it gave a new vocabulary to Pentecostals and charismatics as well as a clinically sound model of ministry that they could use in their churches and ministries. It became a textbook in several schools and a translation in Malayalam has been used in Kerala. A Korean translation is also in use.

After my retirement, I was able to update the book and release it in 2020 and it remains useful to teachers of pastoral care and people involved in caregiving ministries. [By God's grace, we were able to freely distribute copies of this and two other books (*Spiritual Identity and Spirit-Empowered Life* and *What Will Your Tombstone Say?*) to all the major Pentecostal seminaries in Kerala and some outside the state. Copies were given to the library, faculty, and the graduating classes at these institutions. I gratefully acknowledge the assistance we received from *Good News* Chief Editor, C. V. Mathew of Kerala, to accomplish this.]

## Being Oral Roberts' Chaplain

Another unexpected assignment I received was to be the chaplain (prayer partner) for Oral Roberts during some of his visits to the City of Faith as a patient, normally for regular checkups. Visiting Oral Roberts in a medical context to pray for him was another one-of-a-kind experience.

Normally, OR (as he was affectionately referred to internally) was accompanied by a security guard. Unlike many wannabe VIP preachers today who have unnecessary security personnel accompanying them everywhere to guard their egos more than their bodies, Oral Roberts really needed one as there were genuine threats against his life. I would enter his guarded clinic or hospital room and, on most occasions, as soon as he noticed me in my chaplain's gold uniform, he would extend his hand with a smile. I could tell from the kind of handshake and his body language each time if he desired only an immediate prayer or any added dialogue. He believed in the power of prayer and wanted me to focus on that task each time. When I figured out that he did not want an extended dialogue, our exchange was limited to the reason for his visit, concerns on his heart that I could pray about, and not much more. There I was! Praying for the healing of a man who had laid his hands on an estimated two million people and prayed! Once someone asked me what it was like to pray for Oral Roberts' healing. I jokingly told them that it was like praying for Elijah. I never knew exactly how to pray.

December 15, 2009 was a sad day for my family as we received word that Oral Roberts had passed away and joined his beloved wife Evelyn. We attended the funeral services held in the Mabee Center. I was interviewed by Fox News on that day and was quoted in a *Tulsa World* article regarding Oral. As he rests in the presence of the Lord now after a long and fruitful life, I consider my hospital visits with him—when I accompanied him as he prayed for others and when he was the patient—a privilege God had granted me, a preacher's kid from tiny Kerala. I cherish a special handwritten letter from Oral Roberts written to "Dean Matthew" long after he left the campus and his signed portrait now hanging in the hallway of our residence.

A Seminary Dean's Experiment with Servant Leadership

## Oral Over the Ozark

I once had lunch in the City of Faith cafeteria with Rev. Bob DeWeese, Oral Roberts' longtime pilot, faithful associate evangelist, and crusade director. This was the person who preached during the day sessions in the crusade tents, introduced Oral in his unique style and voice as Oral entered the platform, and helped to line up people on the prayer-lines after the sermon. He told me about a time when they were returning from a trip, flying over Arkansas. Unexpectedly, they encountered a terrible storm over the Ozark mountains, and it caused heavy turbulence. The weather conditions got so bad that Bob looked for any airstrip to make a landing. When that became impossible and the plane started to shake violently, Oral told him to crash-land the aircraft in the woods. Bob refused and headed to Tulsa through the storm in spite of Oral's firm requests.

Finally, they landed in Tulsa safely, though badly shaken. Off the plane, DeWeese asked Oral, "Why did you tell me to crash-land? Did the Lord tell you to do so?" Oral replied: "No, the Lord didn't tell me to crash-land. I was just scared!" They laughed together. Bob DeWeese, Oral's faithful associate, learned that God uses His very human servants to accomplish extraordinary things in the world for Him. He recalled Apostle James' word about Prophet Elijah:

> "Elias was a man subject to like passions as we are, and he prayed earnestly that it might not rain: and it rained not on the earth by the space of three years and six months" (James 5:17 KJV).

Thomson K. Mathew

## A Husband and the Bloody Symptom

A physician called me one day and asked me to meet her in a patient's room. I went there and found the doctor with a woman who was admitted because she was coughing up blood. The doctor told me that she could not come up with a proper diagnosis even after a multitude of tests. Tuberculosis to Cancer were all ruled out, but the patient kept spitting up blood. She had no other complaints. The doctor and I spoke with the patient about her life situation. I noticed something unusual as the patient told us her story. I noticed that every time she mentioned her husband, she started coughing and the symptom manifested. I was hesitant to point out my observation, thinking that it may have been just a coincidence, but took a chance and shared my observation with the patient. The doctor and I were surprised to see the patient reacting again the same way.

The doctor told me that she was going to continue her medical care to the best of her ability but recommended that I spend time with this patient in counseling and prayer. I followed up. In that process, I learned the terribly abusive way her husband had been treating her. She told me how she suffered for many years without complaining about her situation, but his cruelty had only increased. Recently the abuse got worse, and she began to have the rare symptom. I kept listening to this woman's story and responded to her pastorally with scripture and prayer. I tried to connect her story (with lower case s) with God's big Story (upper case S) using scripture passages.

To my surprise, after a few sessions, the patient stopped coughing when she mentioned her husband. There was no more dealing with blood. I am sure that the medical care made a difference, but I am also convinced that her condition had a major spiritual component and that the word of God and prayer were also integral to her healing. As a result, she found freedom from bitterness and decided to seek professional Christian counseling back in her community after her discharge. I realized once again that we are fearfully and wonderfully made, and our bodies can react in so many familiar and unfamiliar ways to respond to pain and suffering to send an alarm.

## A Tumor as Big as the Face

Dr. Gene Koelker was the chaplain on a medical/surgical floor in the City of Faith Hospital. One day he called me and other chaplains to join him on his floor to pray for a new patient. It was our protocol to call colleagues to join us for prayer when we faced particularly difficult situations, so it was not unusual to receive such a call. When a call like that came, all we knew was that the chaplain who made the call had run into a difficult situation and needed personal and ministry support from his or her colleagues. Some of us joined Dr. Koelker that day in the patient's room. I noticed that the female patient had a very large tumor on her neck. I had never seen a tumor that big. It was almost as large as her face so that she could not look down! I was getting distracted by the size of the tumor and was moved by the helpless look on the patient's face. Dr. Koelker read a passage from the Bible and anointed the patient with oil and invited us to join him in prayer. [All chaplains at the City of Faith carried small vials of anointing oil to pray for the sick according to James 5:14.] We put all our trust in God and joined in a prayer for healing. Nothing looked different as the prayer ended except that there was a ray of hope in the patient's face. We went back to our units as Dr. Koelker continued his conversation with the patient.

Next morning, we received another call from Chaplain Koelker, asking us to join him in the same patient's room. I was surprised to be called again to the same room but responded. I could not believe what I witnessed in the room. The large tumor was completely gone! Overnight, the tumor had fully disappeared. There was no evidence of the tumor that was left behind except some loose skin around the patient's neck. I do not know what type of medicine was given to her. Neither do I know if I witnessed a miracle of medicine, prayer, or both. All I knew was that I had never seen anything like that tumor disappear that fast. We joined Chaplain Koelker, the patient, and her nurse and thanked God in prayer. I remember the patient being full of joy. She was discharged a few days later.

## Pregnant with Jesus

Once I was called to visit a patient who was admitted because she had claimed that she was pregnant with Jesus. She looked pregnant and from the story she was telling me, it seemed that she belonged in the psychiatric unit. She said that she was pregnant without having any relationship with a man and the only way to make sense of her situation was to believe that God was doing something like what He did with Mary, mother of Jesus.

## A Seminary Dean's Experiment with Servant Leadership

On consultation, our smart doctors told me that she did not belong in the psychiatric floor because she was really sick physically with one of the largest stomach tumors they had seen. This wonderful woman underwent surgery in which a benign tumor reportedly weighing over 50 pounds was removed, and she left the hospital without the story she had depended on to make sense as she fearfully watched her stomach get bigger!

### A Mystery Disease

I had a patient whose symptoms were a mystery to our physicians. It looked like something was literally melting down the patient. The best the doctors could do then was to treat him in the cancer unit. The intensive efforts of our regionally recognized oncologists and other physicians were not producing the desired results.

I visited the patient who was in great suffering but had a very charming personality. He told me of his exciting and adventurous life in many great cities of the world. According to him, it was all paid for by his employer, a major international airline. He also told me that he was a practicing homosexual.

I visited him every day and sat in his room for long periods of time as he had no other visitors. I told him about Jesus and prayed with him on many occasions. He opened his life to Christ, but his symptoms did not improve significantly. He was discharged with only minor progress.

Sometime after his discharge, our doctors told me that they had a newly coined name for the disorder this young airline employee had—Acquired Immune Deficiency

Syndrome (AIDS). They told me what they knew about it then. I was concerned about my health at first as I had taken no precautions against infections when I visited him. I simply washed my hands after holding his hands and praying for him each time as all chaplains are taught to do between visits. I was grateful that I experienced no negative consequences. I do not know what happened to this young man. I hope he lived and the commitment he made to Christ transformed his life.

## "Bring My Father Back!"

Once I was visiting a patient in the Intensive Care Unit. He had been hanging between life and death for several days. The patient's family from out of state was divided in terms of their faith as his wife and a son belonging to the word of faith movement were claiming healing by faith alone and refusing to accept any outcome other than total healing, and the other family members were asking them to release the patient to God. As a chaplain, I was walking theologically very carefully between these two factions. It was as if the patient was waiting to get permission to go to the Lord's presence. He had expressed his faith and hope to me when he was able to speak to me few days earlier. On this day, with the family standing around the patient's bed, I began to pray. Unexpectedly, the wife started to speak to the patient and said that she was selfish to hold on to him and was now ready to release him. "I release you to God, I release you to God," she said. I was really surprised as the heart monitor attached to him began to show a sudden decline of vital numbers after she spoke. As we watched prayerfully and quietly, the patient took his last breath and died in peace.

## A Seminary Dean's Experiment with Servant Leadership

When he realized that his father had just died, the son who had been claiming God's healing jumped out of his seat, rushed toward me, and grabbed my necktie and said in a very loud voice, "We came here for a miracle. Bring my father back, right now." I felt the pressure of his grab but was not choked. I had a flash of fear but said nothing for a few moments. He stood right there staring at me, with his hands still holding my tie.

After a few moments, I gently asked him, "Do you want your dad back just the way he was a few moments ago, or do you want to see him with a new body, with no pain and no tubes hanging on him?" The young man broke down, let go of my tie, and embraced me. I just held him and stood there as he sobbed for a long time. He apologized and sat down. I prayed with the family and stayed to help them make the necessary arrangements to transport the body to their hometown. I never forgot the experience of seeing someone die so soon after a verbal release from a loved one and the grief reaction of a son who loved his dad so dearly that he did not want to let him go.

### Seeing But Blind

I had a patient who was admitted because he reported that he lost his sight. He said that he lost his sight suddenly and could not see anything. I visited him on the day of his admission and listened to his story. He told me about certain painful life events he had experienced and how his sight was lost abruptly. I believed him and prayed with him. The nurse also received the same story.

Then the neurologist came. He spent a significant time with the patient. Other specialists followed. When his healing team met to discuss his case later, I was surprised to hear that the patient had no physical problems with his eyes. His eyes were working perfectly. He had what the doctors called functional blindness. It seemed that the traumas he had experienced had caused this symptom. I do not know all the treatments he received, but he did leave the hospital as a man who could see well.

## Daddy, Am I Dying?

Our daughter Amy used to suffer from childhood asthma. The ragweed in Oklahoma caused her serious allergy problems. One year Amy contracted what was called Asian flu and it affected both her lungs. She was admitted to the Intensive Care Unit of the City of Faith. We had outstanding doctors and healing teams working in the ICU. My friend Dr. David Dunning was the chaplain in the area. He ministered to Amy and to us by visiting us regularly and offering prayer and support. The physicians did everything they could do for her, but her condition was not improving.

One day Amy's heart rate began to rise way above what was considered normal for a child in her condition. The doctor told us that if the condition did not improve within an hour, they would be performing a tracheotomy on her. He explained how a tube would be inserted through her neck to help her receive oxygen to survive.

We stayed in the room, desperately praying for Amy's condition to improve. I noticed that she was trying to say something to me, and I bent down to hear her whisper. She asked me, "Daddy, am I dying?" Obviously, she had picked up our anxiety and was concerned. The question was like an arrow that went through my heart. I told her, "No baby, you are not dying." We continued to pray calmly. Dr. Dunning stood with us. The doctor came in and asked us to wait outside. We waited outside anxiously and were so relieved when the doctor came out and told us that her condition had improved and that she was no longer in need of a tracheotomy! We praised God!

Amy had been healed of her asthma since then as a result of her own faith and prayers by others. Today Amy is a wonderful mother and professional psychologist, but her old question comes to my mind with a tinge of pain and gratitude. As a chaplain at the City of Faith, Amy's heart-breaking question helped me to relate to parents facing such situations and worse ones with a greater measure of compassion.

## Taj Mahal in Agra

The story of Taj Mahal in Agra, India—a monument built by the heartbroken Emperor Sha Jahan to memorialize his untimely deceased beloved wife Mumtaz Mahal—is etched in the Indian psyche, as school children read about it in textbooks and photos of the architectural icon and pride of India are seen everywhere from calendars to textile. It has been my lifelong desire to see the Taj Mahal in Agra, but I never had an opportunity. Finally, Amy and Jamie shared my interest and we decided to stop in Agra during one of our trips to Kerala. We flew to New Delhi, visited my sister Leela who lived there at that time, and traveled by train with her family to Agra. The drastic contrast between the lifestyle of the rich and the life of the poor in India deeply impressed young Amy during our days in New Delhi. Upon return, she wrote an article about a beggar she saw in New Delhi.

It is hard to forget the moment one gets their first glimpse of the Taj Mahal. I have seen several impressive landmark buildings in different parts of the world, but Taj Mahal is the most beautiful building I have ever seen. The uniquely designed white marble structure was larger than I expected. It was more meaningful to me to see the Taj because I had preached about it not being a temple, but a tomb. A summary of the sermon titled, "Temple or Tomb," took a place in my book *Spiritual Identity and Spirit Empowered Life*. Seeing the beautiful structure confirmed the truth of Saint Paul's words undergirding that sermon:

> "Do you not know that your body is the temple of the Holy Spirit *who is* in you, whom you have from God, and you are not your own" (1 Cor 6:19)?

The day we visited Agra was a hot one. As the mercury reached 120 degrees, our kids who were dressed in long Indian outfits began to feel sick. There was no bottled water readily available there in those days and we were not sure about drinking the local water. So we kept drinking Coke which kept increasing our thirst. We decided to spend some hours in a hotel room nearby to cool off and returned to New Delhi from where we flew to Kerala. It was a brief visit, but the memory of Taj Mahal is still alive in all our minds.

## "It's Morning Up Here!"

I had a veteran missionary as a patient. She was over ninety years old when I met her. This godly woman had begun her service in China and was kicked out of that country during the Cultural Revolution. She then went to India and served for a long time in North India until she came back to America some years ago due to failing health. She had a missionary companion with her at the hospital. It was a pleasure to visit this saint. I was encouraged each time I visited her as she shared stories of her service and sacrifices, and of her faith and hope. This was truly a woman of God.

I entered her room one day and saw that the patient was resting in the bed and her companion and a nurse were standing by her side quietly. The nurse hinted that the patient was not doing well. I knew that it was not a moment to have a conversation and joined the two ladies and silently prayed for the missionary with my eyes focused on her face. Suddenly, a big smile came on her face. It really looked like she saw someone she had not seen in a long time. I watched intently as a holy hush fell in the room. Soon her lips began to move. She whispered, "Good night, everyone!"

It was a bright and sunny Oklahoma afternoon. Sunlight was falling into the room through the large windows of the City of Faith hospital room. All three of us looked at each other in reverence of what we had just heard. I noticed that it was not a "Good-bye," but a "Good night!" Her smile returned and she whispered again, "Good night, everyone! It's morning up here!" We knew what she meant, especially as she took her last breath moments after those words.

What a solemn moment! What a privilege to have witnessed it! Yes, she did see her master's face, and smiled. And it seems she took His hand and entered a good morning, after saying "Good night" to us.

After witnessing this home-going, the Lord dealt with me on my fear of death. In my spirit I received a new peace about my own death which has stayed with me since then. It seemed like the Lord taught me that just as my day of birth was preplanned, requiring not much worry or effort on my part, so also is my death pre-appointed and I do not need to worry too much about it as I will not be the main actor on that day. And certainly, I will be going to a better place that day than the one to which my birth brought me.

## Will You Remember Me?

I met a beautiful young lady as a patient in the City of Faith Hospital on the cancer unit. She was suffering from breast cancer. She was a born-again Christian who had no family members to visit her. Her mother and grandmother had died from breast cancer, her father was also dead, and she had no siblings. She lived alone and kept her sickness a secret without seeking medical help as long as she could, due to fear. According to the doctors, her prognosis was not good because by the time she came to the hospital, the disease had progressed significantly.

I visited her daily, listened to her stories, and prayed with her. Despite the heroic efforts made by the dedicated medical staff, her condition grew worse. One day during a pastoral visit she asked me, "I have no family left. I don't know how long I will live. Can I ask you for a favor?"

Thinking that she would ask for some practical help, I said, "Of course. What can I do for you?"

She asked, "Would you remember me once I am gone?"

Moved by her unexpected request, I said, "Certainly. I will remember you." I also told her about the Lord who will remember her forever as He has carved her in the palm of His hands!

That was our last visit.

## Healing Ministry Does Not End

After the announcement regarding the closing of the City of Faith, it took some time to transfer the medical students to other schools based on American Medical Association rules and pay off faculty contracts before the facility could be closed. It had been my privilege to visit the first hospital patient and pray with that adult female in 1981 and in 1989 I was able to pray with the last patient, an infant in the Intensive Care Unit. As I was leaving the City of Faith Hospital for the last time, I had an impression in my heart that although the City of Faith was being closed, the healing ministry of Jesus would continue through the graduates of Oral Roberts University, and particularly through the graduates of the ORU School of Theology and Missions (name then).

*Chapter 8*

# Stories From ORU

## Pray, Doc, Pray

I began my administrative service in the seminary as dean of students and director of field education. The duties of the dean of students included facilitating fellowship among seminary students. Following the path of the previous dean of students, I used to organize potluck (some called it potbless) dinners for seminarians and families. I recall one occasion when we had a fellowship dinner on a weekend night. Each seminarian was supposed to bring at least one dish sufficient to feed four people. Normally, there would be enough food to feed everyone as each student or family, although they were generally on low budgets, brought a main dish, a salad, vegetables, desserts, or something else. Normally the available food had enough of each. This night was different. Only a few main dishes were brought in, and the line of hungry students was much longer than usual.

Student leaders began to place the food items on several tables but kept looking at me as the line of students got longer and longer. Students in the front of the line filled their plates as if there was no shortage. A tall seminarian from the back of the line kept shouting to me saying, "You'd better pray, doc. You'd better pray, doc." As the tables were getting empty and we were running out of even paper plates, students kept looking at me like I was going to multiply the food, just like Jesus did. The student in the back started shouting louder, "You'd better pray, doc. You'd better pray, doc!"

I knew I was in trouble and ran to my car. I took off to the nearest grocery store, Bud's on Lewis Avenue where the Office Depot now stands, ran in, and started grabbing anything I could find that could be eaten immediately, and more paper plates and napkins. Shoppers there looked at me like I was a mad man. I stood anxiously on the checkout line worrying that it would be too late by the time I got back to campus.

I did get back before the hungry students disappeared and the student leaders put the items I brought from the store on a table as fast as they could. There was a lot of bread! The fellow who was shouting "you'd better pray, doc," just looked at me with a huge smile. Every time I saw him on campus after that night, we greeted each other, saying, "you'd better pray, doc." I changed the fellowship dinner procedure after that experience and made sure that the school supplied the main items and students were expected to bring only the side dishes.

# A Seminary Dean's Experiment with Servant Leadership

## Only 3,000 Dollars

Dr. Roy Hayden was a distinguished scholar and an outstanding teacher who was involved in producing the original New International Version of the Bible. He was a respected professor who loved ORU and was willing to do anything to assist his students. He had a special concern for international students. He gave financial assistance from his personal funds to many students in need. He took up a project to increase the amount he could donate. When recycling was not even a well-known concept, Dr. Hayden collected soda cans from various areas of the campus, sold them by weight, and gave the money to needy students. One could see Dr. Hayden, a respected senior professor, walking around with a bag and collecting the soda cans from every part of the campus. Walking was his lifestyle. He lived in a house close to the campus and walked to work regularly. He also had some international students living in his house from time to time.

When I was serving as dean of students in the seminary, a student came to my office seeking some additional scholarship funds. I listened to him to understand his financial situation and to determine how much additional money he needed. I asked him what caused the shortfall but was disappointed to hear his answer. He said, "I am here because Dr. Hayden gave me only $3,000!" I was sad that this student could not appreciate the sacrifices behind the $3,000. He did not seem to be interested in any details, but I did help him to stay in school.

I am sad to report that this intellectually smart student did graduate from ORU Seminary and became a pastor, but just a short time later, I learned that he was voted out of two congregations and was in the market looking for another church to pastor. I do not know the real cause of his dismissals but wonder if a lack of gratitude was one of the causes of his troubles.

I do not know what happened to him since then. I now recall what Professor Maurice Culver told me in my office on his last day at ORU—after his retirement party—when I asked him of his feelings on that day, at the end of a lifetime of distinguished service to God. He told me that one word could summarize all his emotions—"Grateful!"

## A Repenting Student

A seminary dean deals with all sorts of unexpected student problems. I was no exception. I had to deal with a church's unusual complaint about one of our students who was their former pastor. They claimed that he stole several pieces of expensive furniture from their parsonage. I had to respond to a wife once who wanted me to force her former husband to pay child support. Some did not realize that although I could discipline them or try to discharge them, legally I had no jurisdiction over certain aspects of their lives. Most students responded to correction. Some would not. Sometimes I have seen real transformations taking place during their studies. The following demonstrates a case of transformation that took place after a student left the campus without completing his studies.

## A Seminary Dean's Experiment with Servant Leadership

The letter below from a former student represents God's work in a person's life after making a mistake. I have withheld his name.

Dr. Thomson Mathew
College of Theology and Ministry
Oral Roberts University
7777 S. Lewis Ave., Tulsa, OK 74171
(Zip code, corrected by author)

Dr. Mathew,

I am a former student who recently withdrew from the Graduate Theology program. I left school to pursue a ministry opportunity and I would like to thank you for being willing to allow me to do so. I would also like to seek your forgiveness.

While a student at Oral Roberts University, I maintained a high grade point average but neglected to learn everything I needed to know. I've participated in many spiritual formation activities, but never managed to reach maturity. I had many opportunities to build relationships, but I left with a few true lifelong friendships. I squandered the gift God gave me and left ORU no different but rather worse than when I arrived.

In general, I had a very poor attitude that prevented me from growing as a student, Christian, and minister. I thought I knew everything and sought to use the seminary experience merely as an opportunity to earn a certification for service. I watched countless colleagues flourish in their spiritual and emotional lives while my own withered into darkness. I left ORU bitter, divisive, and hateful.

In retrospect, I was unkind toward fellow students, disrespectful of instructors and administrators, and unfairly critical of our institution. Most of all, I was disobedient toward my Lord. In the end, my place that (sic) ORU could have been filled by an individual who would have fully appreciated the opportunity.

Please forgive me for being such a disruptive student and reflecting so purely on you, ORU, and Jesus Christ. I know that God called me to earn a masters degree from ORU and -- after some time of restoration -- I would like to reapply for admission, but I will not do so until my attitude is right. Until I can love others the way He loves me, I will not be fully ready to step into His calling on my life.

Thank you for your ministry and heart for service toward your faculty, staff, and students.

Sincerely,

(Name withheld)

## A President on His Knees

Once Dr. Jerry Horner, Dr. Dan Hedges, and I had a meeting in President Richard Roberts' office. Just days before we went up to his office, Dr. Hedges, director of the DMin program, who had been suffering from pain in his foot was told that he was dealing with something serious which needed to be examined by the oncologists at M. D. Anderson Hospital in Houston. Our meeting took place the day before he was scheduled to fly down to M.D. Anderson Hospital for follow up and final diagnosis. As we finished our business with the president, all of us still seated, Dan Hedges told the president about his medical situation. Suddenly, Richard Roberts, the president of the university, got down on his knees and gently grabbed Dan's foot with both hands and started praying for his healing.

As the president knelt on the floor, Dr. Horner and I jumped up and stood as Dan remained seated. I was moved by seeing Richard Roberts and his heart for healing which persuaded him to be on his knees to hold the foot of an associate with his bare hands and pray. That moment in which I saw his sense of calling to the healing ministry and the spirit in which he fulfilled that call remains with me.

I am happy to report that Dan Hedges did make that scheduled trip to M. D. Anderson Hospital and returned with a report saying that he had no cancer. We do not know if he was healed of cancer, but we do know that his doctors in Tulsa had very good reasons to send him to Houston. In any case, I was glad to bear witness to a second-generation healing evangelist's heart for healing revealed in a very private setting.

## Swearing in DMin Class

Before I became dean, we had two groups of DMin students every semester—a modular group that came to campus for two weeks at a time and a Monday-only group that came to classes one day at a time each semester. Most of the modular students came from out of town and stayed in a hotel. Pastors from the local region drove in on Mondays,

*141*

considered a day off for many pastors. We decided to discontinue the Monday-only program and merge these two groups to save faculty time and brought the two cohorts together to campus for two weeks. Unfortunately, each group felt that it was academically superior to the other and this feeling started manifesting in the class in different ways.

We used to coteach two DMin courses in ten days and at certain times there could be up to four professors, including the director, in the class. In one session where Drs. Charles Snow, Kenneth Mayton, Ed Decker and I were present, we gave the students—all mature ministers—an opportunity to discuss their feelings about being brought together as one group. Students began to share their feelings. Things got so wound up that at one point a highly respected minister from one group jumped off his seat and shouted a terrible swear word at another student from the other group. We were stunned. I ran to close the doors to prevent people in the hallway from hearing the language in the pastors' DMin class, and to prevent our potential termination by Dean Chappell. Things did calm down and the student who lost his temper and swore apologized, and that group of ministers turned out to be one of the best cohorts of ORU DMin graduates. Some of them serve God today in very distinguished positions.

## Holy Hush in MDiv Class

It was my habit as dean to walk by the classrooms on the fourth floor of the Graduate Center during class hours. Most Theology classes were held on the fourth floor. As we had outstanding professors who were Spirit-filled scholars,

## A Seminary Dean's Experiment with Servant Leadership

I had no worry about the content of their teaching but walking around the hallways gave me a sense of the tone of things in the classes. For instance, at one time some students complained that a teacher was turning his classroom into a revival service and was not covering the academic topics required by the syllabus. I had to call the attention of that professor to the students' concern.

One day I was in the hallway and went by a class with a slightly open door. I saw a couple of students on the floor, and no sound was coming out of the class. Curious, I opened the door slightly and found that the entire class, including the professor, was on the floor. I noticed the professor sitting silently, leaning against the wall. I sensed a holy hush and stepped back without causing a distraction, closed the door, and went back to my office. I learned later that while Dr. Henry Lederle, a globally recognized scholar, was giving a lecture on the Holy Spirit, a divine presence was felt by everyone in the room and a holy hush came on them. All they could do was to simply sit down on the floor and soak in the presence of God. I do not know how that session ended but was sure that there were not many ATS seminaries where this type of teaching and learning took place.

### Olympic Gold Medalist Becomes Chaplain

Madeline Manning Mims is an Olympic Gold Medalist in track. She won the Gold Medal in the 800-meter run and held the Olympic Record, World Record, and American Record for this item for 15 years. She was a member of four Olympic Teams, inducted into the National and Olympic

Halls of Fame, and was named one of America's Outstanding Young Women. I have heard her speak in chapel as a guest but was surprised to get a call from her one day, asking for an appointment to meet me. I had no idea what an Olympic Gold Medalist had to tell me.

Madeline came to my office and shared a huge vision with me. She told me about her efforts to minister to the Olympians and the difficulties she was running into due to her lack of internationally recognized credentials to be a chaplain. She said God was calling her to start an international chaplaincy ministry to the Olympians and other world class athletes. Madeline was a graduate of Tennessee State University with a degree in Sociology but lacked formal theological education at that time. Her global vison was huge, and I was not sure if she would be willing to make the long and rigorous academic and clinical journey required to get where she wanted to go. I told her about her need to earn a Master of Divinity and complete clinical training to become certified as a fully credentialed chaplain. I promised her anything I could do to assist her.

I should have remembered that I was talking to an Olympic Gold Medalist, a person who did not back off from challenges! Madeline enrolled in the Master of Divinity program and graduated with impressive grades, but she did not stop. She enrolled in our Doctor of Ministry program and graduated. We met many times during her student days to review her progress. All I did was just cheer her from the sidelines.

Dr. Madeline Mims paid the academic price fully, unlike many others I have advised during my tenure, and went through the required clinical pastoral training. Meanwhile, she established the United States Council for Sports Chaplaincy (USCSC). I was an advisor to her and the organization until I retired from ORU. She continues to minister to the Olympians and other high-level athletes who face tremendous pressures personally and trains world-class athletes in sports chaplaincy through the USCSC.

What an amazing woman of God! What a privilege it has been for me to know her as an Olympic-quality minister of the Gospel who can sing, preach, counsel, pray, and educate!

## Two Valedictorians

I was the associate dean of the seminary when both of my daughters were roommates on campus and I became dean during Amy's last semester at ORU. On chapel days when there was a guest speaker who caught their special attention, they used to come by my office to discuss their experience with me. When I spoke in chapel, we used to go off campus to have lunch together away from everyone. Both finished their baccalaureate degrees in three years. It was incredibly stressful for them. If I knew then what I know now, I would have asked them to take their time and finish their degrees in four years.

Jamie was on campus on 9/11. The entire campus community gathered in chapel on that day and some of us led the gathering in prayer. Jamie mentioned that day of prayer in her 2002 graduation speech. Amy was selected as valedictorian in 2000 through a competition among the schools as usual. When Jamie was selected, President Richard Roberts and a special committee had to give additional approval of her selection because I was a dean, as they did not want to give the impression that somehow my deanship gave her the title. The proudest days for Molly and me at ORU were the graduation days of our daughters when each one brought an audience of 10,000 people to their feet as they finished their speeches. Amy's speech was outstanding, and Jamie's was also one-of-a-kind. For years after their commencements, valedictorians were measured by the oratory standard they set. Jamie's speech was also used as a recruiting tool for several years. The manuscripts of their speeches are included in the Appendix.

## Ervin and Mansfield: Professors First, Advisors Later

Dr. Howard M. Ervin was a confidant of Oral Roberts and was involved in the establishment of the Theology program from the beginning of ORU, even before the formation of a graduate seminary. A Baptist pastor with a PhD from Princeton who was filled with the Holy Spirit, he was a formidable person and scholar. He debated with world class scholars on the baptism of the Holy Spirit and was involved in the Catholic-Pentecostal dialogue. He was well known and highly respected in the Pentecostal/charismatic world. He taught pneumatology in the seminary for decades. He retired at least twice and was invited back to teach classes every time. Dr. Ervin had such a vocabulary that even students whose native language was English used to bring their dictionaries to class to grasp what he was saying. His book, *These are not Drunken as You Suppose* (title changed later to *Spirit-Baptism*) was highly acclaimed. He was the one Oral Roberts called when he had a question on the Old Testament before preaching a sermon or writing a manuscript.

Dr. Ervin was my pneumatology professor in the DMin program. The course was demanding, and we were required to write a major paper at the end of the course. Unfortunately, I had to make a trip to India and had to submit my paper way before the deadline. I wrote a good paper with sufficient footnotes, but in my rush, submitted it without a bibliography attached. He liked the paper but gave me a B grade, saying that he did not give A grades to papers without a bibliography, notwithstanding the foreign trip and early submission. There was no option to submit a bibliography later. This is a silly topic today, but in my mindset as an employee/student on tuition benefit then, a B was a real disappointment.

When Dr. Chappell recommended me to the faculty years later, Dr. Ervin was my strong advocate along with Dr. Larry Lacour and Dr. Robert Mansfield, my professors of preaching and New Testament, respectively. A decade after I became a professor, God showed His sense of humor by appointing me as the dean of these giants of faith. By then, Dr. Lacour had retired, Dr. Mansfield became a distinguished professor and recognized Methodist preacher in the area, and Dr. Ervin began to read quantum physics for fun! In some faculty meetings where Dr. Ervin spoke, we struggled to grasp the theological insights he was gaining from quantum physics!

When certain situations confronted me as dean and I needed counsel, I used to go to Dr. Ervin's office. His best advice often was, "This is only a blip on God's screen, Tom. Don't worry about it." Years after, I was honored when he invited me to write the preface to his book, *Healing: Sign of the Kingdom*. Based on his request, his family asked two of his disciples to speak at his funeral—Dr. James Barber and me. Dr. Barber also had a fatherly relationship with Dr. Ervin. What a saint he was! What a legacy he has left behind!

Dr. Robert Mansfield became another valued advisor to me when I became dean. He was a regular participant in our informal lunchroom discussions. It was a privilege to meet with him privately in my office on many occasions to pray together.

## The Disciple-Colleagues

The list of Theology graduates who have become great leaders internationally is long. We made a partial list of such individuals once, especially those in the US. Some of the best graduates of the college went on for advanced learning and returned to teach in their alma mater. These include current and former professors, including Drs. Paul Chappell, Larry Hart [I saw a copy of Dr. Hart's *Truth Aflame* on a bookshelf in a pastor's office in the Czech Republic!], James and Sally Shelton, Samuel Thorpe, Jeffrey Lamp, Cheryl Iverson, Edward Watson, James Barber, Timothy Ekblad, Raymond Smith, Bill Buker, William McDonald, Kerry Loescher, William Lyons, Sandra Richardson, John Thompson, Andrea Walker, Kelly James, Jeffrey Voth, Christopher Foster, and Daniel Bunn. Dr. Cheryl Iverson, Dr. Ed Watson, Dr. Sam Thorpe, and Dr. Christopher Foster have served as outstanding department chairs for extended periods of time. Dr. Paul Chappell served as Dean for eight years and Sam Thorpe served as an Interim Dean. The continuing service of former students guarantees the preservation of ORU's DNA.

Dr. James Barber was Rev. Larry Lea's (who served as dean of the seminary before Dr. Chappell) associate at Church on the Rock in Dallas. He enrolled in the MDiv program at ORU and attended my pastoral care classes. He earned the MDiv and while serving as men's pastor at Victory Christian Church in Tulsa, completed his DMin. Later, he got involved in CPE and became a hospice chaplain. I hired him to teach pastoral care courses and to lead the field education program. After I retired, he became director of the DMin program. He tells me and his students how his life changed in my class. Dr. Barber has been a true disciple. He was my student, then my colleague, additionally on two occasions he served on review committees chaired by Hillcrest Hospital CPE Supervisor Dr. Jacob George for my recertification as a Board Certified Chaplain (BCC).

I maintained the BCC certification even though I did not work as a professional chaplain to assist our students who were interested in chaplaincy. I wanted more Pentecostal/charismatic ministers to enter this field of ministry in the military and other institutions because historically chaplaincy has been dominated by non-Pentecostal clergy. Because of this desire, I was supportive of the Chaplaincy for Full Gospel Churches (CFGC), the premiere agency formally endorsing chaplains from independent charismatic churches to serve in the military. I have led continuing education sessions for US military chaplains organized by CFGC.

As I mentioned earlier, I had the privilege of being Dr. Ervin's student, then his colleague, and later his dean. My own disciples James Barber (now DMin director), Bill Buker (current associate dean), and Tim Ekblad (director of the modular/distance education program), and others are now passing on the ORU DNA.

## Where I Did Not Go

There is one place I never visited despite multiple invitations. It is Fiji. When I received the first invitation to teach at a native school there during the summer, Fiji was recoiling from a coup with much tension in the population between native Fijians and East Indians who made up almost half of the population. The deposed prime minister was the first East Indian elected to that office. There has been a long history of bloody strife between the two populations due to Fiji's history of indentured Indian labor under the British rule. I was advised not to go to Fiji at such a time. I thought the solution was to send Dr. James Barber, an African American, who did not have to worry about the race issue there!

Dr. Barber did a great job in Fiji and Dr. Raymond Smith, professor of missions, joined him during subsequent visits. They kept long hours teaching native pastors at different locations during each visit, often outdoors in the hot climate, making frequent inter-island trips. Dr. Barber has joked saying that he had to rescue Dean Mathew who was afraid to go where God called him!

## Sound of a Click

We had an international student who served as a student worker in the DMin office. Those were the days when each department had to keep track of the money spent on long distance phone calls. We were very careful not to exceed the budget designated for this expense and normally the cost stayed within the budget. This changed suddenly. We began to see large amounts charged for international calls made from the DMin office. Although we had international contacts from that office, the large amount spent on unusually long calls did not make sense. Normally, the admissions office or the dean's office dealt with international matters.

As the amount kept increasing month after month, we decided to investigate. It turned out that the calls were being made to a couple of numbers in a particular foreign nation. We became curious as the student worker in the area was from that nation. The student's extension did not show up in the phone reports, only the main number for the DMin area was on them.

Dr. Mayton, the director of the DMin program, and I met with the student and told him about our observation and asked him if he was making such calls. He denied vehemently. We knew that the coincidence was too much for such long conversations to take place with someone in the student's homeland by anyone else in the department.

I told the student that lying about it was more troublesome to me than the actual issue because I could understand a homesick student calling home using what he thought might be a free call from a place of work. He kept denying until I said that if he did not tell me the truth, the next sound he would hear would be the click of an airplane seatbelt. He looked shocked and confessed that he had been coming back to the office after hours and was calling his mother and a girlfriend back home. He then apologized. We forgave him and told him he could not continue to call them from the work phone anymore. Dr. Mayton reminds me of the "click of the seatbelt" statement from time to time.

## Meeting Rev. Kenneth Copeland's Family

One of the successful programs we implemented in the seminary was a continuing education program for pastors in the Pentecostal/charismatic movement. They were widely publicized, and many pastors and well-known ministers attended these learning sessions. We chose relevant topics and had the best faculty teach those subjects. We had interactive sessions and delightful lunches during these courses. These were clearly defined continuing education courses that did not claim regular academic credit. We gave certificates of completion to all participants.

Many pastors attended all the non-credit courses offered and, appreciating what the seminary had to offer through these courses, some enrolled in the academic degree programs later. Through the continuing education program, we got to know Evangelist Kenneth Copeland's daughter Terri and her husband George Pearsons. They attended several courses and kept a close connection with me and the seminary.

I was invited to the Kenneth Copeland Ministry (KCM) campus in Fort Worth to spend a day with their staff and to teach a seminar on pastoral care. That was a delightful experience which allowed me to get to know the Copeland family more personally. I heard many family stories that day, including some from the time when Rev. Copeland was Oral

Roberts' pilot. I was aware that Oral Roberts had his own zip code in Tulsa but was impressed with the scope of the Copeland Ministry. [Because of ORU's exclusive zip code, I have received letters with only my name and the zip code written on it.]

## Carlton Pearson Comes Out

Carlton Pearson, former ORU student and Tulsa pastor, was like a son to Oral Roberts. He was a gifted singer and a great preacher, and his church, Higher Dimension, was growing rapidly and enjoyed a great reputation in Tulsa. He was also traveling all around the world and preaching with the church as his home base. There were other ministers on his staff who took care of the pastoral needs of the congregation while he traveled. One of our professors in the undergraduate area invited Carlton as a guest speaker in his class. While the class was going on, a student from the class came running to my office and told me that Carlton was teaching some very strange doctrines. It turned out that what Carlton said in class was a version of universalism.

The news about Carlton's class lecture reached President Richard Roberts within minutes and he called me to check things out. I tried to find out what really happened in the class from the recently hired professor who had invited Carlton to speak. He was not much help at that time as he told me that precisely at the time Carlton said certain things, he had stepped out of the class!

Soon Carlton announced his new theological position publicly and it was a big controversy. Oral Roberts wrote a long letter to Carlton admonishing him to give up the teaching and sent a copy of that letter to me. It was such an appealing letter as if it were written by a father to his son, trying to persuade Carlton to give up his new teaching, reminding him that as he was a very gifted speaker, he could mislead a great number of people.

Carlton did not take the counsel and continued to spread his new teachings. His church was closed, and he left Tulsa. I learned that he got involved with a church in Chicago that required the clergy to have a seminary degree. I tried to recruit him to our graduate program to assist him, hoping to influence him through the faculty, and had several conversations with him but was not successful in getting him enrolled.

## Sleepless in Moscow

During our stay in Moscow where Dr. Jernigan and I had gone with the team from Livets Ord University, we had a scary experience one night. Dr. Jernigan and I were staying in adjacent rooms at a nice hotel away from the meeting place. Late one night, we had a knock on our doors and as we opened the doors, we were asked to give our passports to the people who looked official but did not identify themselves. The procedure to enter the country at the airport was already intimidating, as Jernigan and I with our US passports had to go through certain lines and face certain questions with intense looks, so we were both apprehensive about surrendering our passports to the people who knocked on our doors late at night, especially because we had already shown our passports at the hotel counter as we registered and they had made copies of our documents. Having heard certain horror stories, our concern was that we may not see the passports again and there would be no way to show who we were, why we were there, when we came, and so forth if the authorities chose to consider treating us in an unfriendly way.

We spent a few sleepless hours in our rooms and were extremely happy to hear the knock again when the same people brought our passports back. We never knew why they wanted to take our passports from us late that night but remain grateful that our stay there and our exit went smoothly. Our hosts in Russia took good care of us and fed us both local and international foods. At the end of the conference, they took us to a musical in the famous Bolshoi Opera Theater. What a privilege it was for me to minister together in Russia with ORU's beloved Dr. J. who began his ministry with Oral Roberts during the days of his tent crusades!

## A High School Student Translator

During Richard Roberts' presidency, a major healing crusade was held in El Salvador. Two Spanish-speaking students spearheaded the efforts to have the seminarians from ORU participate in this mission led by the university president. One was Adrian Compton, an accomplished singer and a regular worship leader in chapel and on Richard's TV program, and another was Edgar Gonzalez, an attorney from Puerto Rico who completed a DMin degree at ORU. The travel group included other students, including Joy Ames, who later earned a PhD from Asbury Seminary.

It was a beautiful experience as Molly and I traveled with the students to El Salvador and preached the gospel, visited orphanages, and prayed for so many people during our stay there. El Salvador was a dangerous place for foreigners, and we had extra security at the hotel where we stayed. Everywhere we went security people carrying big guns accompanied us. I have never forgotten one security woman who was less than 5 feet tall carrying a big gun accompanying us. She did not inspire confidence, but then again, I did not see her respond to a real threat. Richard Roberts preached there in the night services, and I preached in the day meetings.

One day Dr. Gonzalez was translating for me. In the middle of the message, he lost his voice completely and the only person in the large gathering who could help me was a young high school student who was studying English as a second language with hopes of studying in a college in the United States. She agreed to help me to finish the message. She stepped up and did an outstanding job. God really moved in all the meetings in El Salvador.

We also preached at a couple of local churches. At one church, at the end of the message, we saw an older lady well over 70 years old at the altar, marching like a soldier. It was like a spiritual battle was taking place right before our eyes in that gang-filled area and the old woman of God was winning it. I have never forgotten that trip and the impact this missionary work had upon us and our students.

Another surprise we had in El Salvador was an earthquake we experienced there, which was milder than the one I had experienced years earlier in Van Nyes while teaching at the ORU extension at Church on the Way. We were told by

## A Seminary Dean's Experiment with Servant Leadership

our hosts in El Salvador not to worry about it and we went on with our schedule.

As mentioned, Joy Ames graduated from ORU and went on to earn her PhD from Asbury Theological Seminary. Adrian Compton became a pastor in San Antonio, Texas. He invited us to his church a year ago to conduct a seminar, preach at the church, and to dedicate his baby. We had a wonderful time with Adrian's family and his church. Dr. Gonzalez is now pastoring the Hispanic congregation at SpiritLife Church, the former Evangelistic Temple in Tulsa, where the Oral Roberts family has long roots.

### One Clue in Atlanta

I flew to Atlanta to attend a conference. My administrative assistant Judy Cope had made all the travel arrangements. She had a gift of minding details which was a great blessing to me. I never experienced an unpleasant surprise at my destinations, domestic or international, if Judy had made the arrangements.

I landed in Atlanta, picked up my baggage, and took a door-to-door service van to go to my hotel which happened to be the last stop. I had placed my baggage in the back compartment with everyone else's and patiently sat in my seat to get to the hotel. I was shocked to get off the van at my destination and discover that the only bag left in the compartment was not mine and it had no name or address on it.

Obviously, someone had taken my bag and got off at another hotel and I had no idea who or where. The van driver took off without offering any help. I was really concerned and did not know how I would get my bag back. I called Judy in a crisis mode. She asked me to look through the contents of the bag and see if there were any personally identifiable items in it. Fortunately, the bag was unlocked, and I was able to check the contents carefully. There was nothing identifiable in it except a bottle of prescribed medicine. There was a name on the bottle but no contact information except the name of a pharmacy. I gave the information to Judy.

Judy hunted for a phone number for the pharmacy and got it. She called the pharmacy, but the pharmacist could not give her any information on the named person due to the federal laws regarding medical privacy. The pharmacist told her that the medicine was for a major cardiac issue and that the patient must take it within a certain time. He said that the man who had my bag was in worse trouble than I was. Judy persuaded the pharmacist to call the wife of the man and had her call her husband who would call me. Fortunately, the lady was at home when the pharmacist called, and I was so relieved to get that call from the owner of the bag.

My companion in misery volunteered to bring my bag to my hotel. He kept his word, and we were the happiest strangers who ever met! Judy called back to check on the status of things and to remind me that what she did that day was not on her ORU job description! I hope this story illustrates what a great and creative team I was blessed to have as dean.

## Story of Two Special Bags

After I stepped down from deanship, we decided to downsize and move to a smaller residence, but I did not expect downsizing to be as hard as it turned out to be. I had a

## A Seminary Dean's Experiment with Servant Leadership

collection of souvenirs from more than a hundred cities I had visited and other things with emotional attachments, and I found it hard to decide what to keep and what to donate. We concluded that we needed help. Thankfully, the Community Education department of Jenks High School offered a timely course on downsizing! We enrolled and attended the class. We received some practical help from the course and resumed our effort. We let go of a lot of things, much with a deep sense of loss. We really did not know how much "stuff" we had accumulated! Much of it was not junk.

A truck came from Habitat for Humanity and picked up furniture. Another one came from the Salvation Army and picked up appliances and other things. We made several trips to the local Goodwill collection center. I had a personal library at the office and one at home. I had already decided to donate my personal academic library to enhance the educational programs at India Bible College and Seminary in Kerala, and to honor the ministries of my parents and grandparents. ORU staff member and seminary graduate Rejani Joseph's husband Chakko Joseph helped us to pack and ship the books based on the requirements at the port of entry in India. Chakko Joseph considers it his ministry to build up theological libraries at Bible schools in developing nations.

While we let go of many materially and emotionally valuable things, we kept two old bags. These were the bags Molly and I brought to America on our first trips here, I in 1972 and Molly in 1975. We filled them with some memorable things like the dresses our daughters wore when they were dedicated to God as infants. We plan to give one box to each child to make sure that they remember that when we came to America, all our earthly goods could be contained in these two bags. America has been good to us. Whatever we now own or hold, from advanced degrees to finances, are gifts of opportunities America gave us. Although our daughters already live as they know this well, we do not want them to be tempted to forget this testimony after we are no longer here.

## Looking for a Missing Student

A couple of unusual experiences I had during my service at Oral Roberts University have made me realize the importance of the need for the guidance of the Holy Spirit in our lives. One incident stands out which took place during my work as the dean of students. I had an impression one day to check on a student whom I had not seen for several days. I checked with several professors to see if they had seen her and learned that she was not attending their classes. I considered leaving the thought alone but felt persuaded to check on her well-being.

In those days, ORU owned an apartment complex for graduate students across Lewis Avenue. I called the manager of the apartment complex and inquired if she had seen this seminary student. She also had not seen her in several days. I became more concerned and asked the manager to check on her. She asked me to come along with her and I went across the street to the apartment complex and met the manager.

We went to the student's apartment together. The manager used her master key to unlock the apartment's front door. As she opened the door, to our shock and surprise we saw the student lying on the floor behind the door fully unconscious.

We called 911 and she was taken to the hospital. It was learned later that she was a diabetic and was in a hypoglycemic coma. The paramedics told us that if we had not called when we did, her life would have been lost. I was glad to see the student return to classes and complete the school year.

## A Flight and God's Deadline

I was returning from a speaking engagement in Palm Springs and settling down in my seat on my connecting flight in Dallas, eager to get home on a Sunday night. The short flight was scheduled to arrive in Tulsa by 10 PM. A young lady who looked somewhat distressed took the seat next to me and started a conversation. Basically, she was telling me a story. She was a student at the University of Oklahoma and had her specific plans for her future, but recently felt in her spirit that she was called to earn a master's degree in counseling and enter a counseling ministry. She felt impressed to enroll in the MA in Christian Counseling degree program at Oral Roberts University.

This would be a big decision, and finances were such a concern that the young woman said she needed a real confirmation of her inner impression. She went on a visit to her friends in the Northeast to discuss this change of plans, hoping that they would provide her the confirmation she sought. She was on her way back without receiving the confirmation. She mentioned that she told the Lord that if she did not receive a reliable confirmation before 10 PM that day, she would forget the idea of becoming a Christian counselor.

I was intrigued and amused by her story but kept listening to her without saying anything about my position at ORU. I noticed that the distress on her face was increasing as we began our descent to the Tulsa area. As we approached the runway just few minutes before 10 PM, I told the young lady that I was the dean of the graduate school where the MA in Christian Counseling degree was housed and if she enrolled, I would look for some extra scholarship money for her. I will never forget her look. Her jaws dropped and she sat like a tableau for a few moments. Soon the tears started flowing. She had received the confirmation she was seeking!

I am glad to report that she did enroll at ORU, studied counseling, and became a counselor. I have asked her to speak to several incoming classes of students regarding the need to be guided by the Holy Spirit into their calling.

## Call on Monday

The status of the DMin program was a major concern when Dr. Jerry Horner left the deanship and Dr. Dan Hedges, whom he had brought to direct the DMin, was considering a shift in ministry. I needed to make a change in leadership and called Dr. Ken Mayton to see if he would return to campus to become director of the program. I was hoping to get both Dr. Charles Snow and Dr. Kenneth Mayton who had left ORU to pastor churches back on the faculty. I wanted it especially because I knew their quality of teaching and capacity for mentoring students in the seminary.

Being a senior pastor at a mega church in California, Dr. Mayton was not open to the idea of moving back to Tulsa

## A Seminary Dean's Experiment with Servant Leadership

when I first approached him, but I kept calling him. I almost gave up but called him once again on a Monday morning and he agreed to return. I have a hypothesis about preachers and Mondays—that most pastors feel emotionally down on Mondays after a demanding Sunday, especially those with churches that have multiple services, and that pastors are more open to consider other forms of ministry on Mondays!

Dr. Mayton and I have laughed about my hypothesis. My Monday morning call paid off and Dr. Mayton and his wife Judith returned to campus where he served as director of the DMin program, and Judith served as a faculty member in the department of Psychology. Dr. Snow also returned as professor of preaching and leadership in the seminary and directed the Ministry Training and Development Institute (MTDI), a lay training program we initiated when Dr. Frank Hultgren was faculty chaplain. The ORU Bible Institute currently directed by our seminary graduate Sam Barsoum now continues the legacy of MTDI as a valuable certificate and diploma program.

## Some Great Pastors

I met some outstanding pastors in different parts of the world during my tenure at ORU. I will name just a few of these shepherds who made a big difference in their communities and served as our prayer partners from time to time, including some who have gone to be with the Lord. ORU Seminary graduates Steve Boyce of New Life Church in Rhode Island and Pastor Michael McAfee of Iowa; ORU graduate and former chaplain Bill Shuler of Washington, DC;

Rev. M. S. Samuel, a leader of the first Pentecostal church of Indian immigrants in New York City, and Rev. K. V. Kurian who followed him; Pastors John C. Daniel, Abraham Samuel, and A. C. George who invited me and Professor E. Samkutty of Louisiana to get involved in ministry among the "American Born Keralites" (ABK's); Pastors Oommen Abraham and Jacob Cherian who led the founding of the Pentecostal Conference of North American Keralites (PCNAK); Pastors John Thomas and K. C. John who labored for Christ among Keralite immigrants in South Florida; Pastors Armon Newburn, H. A. Brummett, and Jamie Austin of Woodlake Assembly in Tulsa; Dr. Mark Merrill of Georgia; Rev. Robert (Bob) Wise of Massachusetts, and Pastors Greg Ables and Chris Beasley who lead Newspring Family Church in Jenks are just a few of these shepherds.

Others in this group are ORU DMin graduates. Their list includes Pastor Billy Joe Dougherty, whose class paper from a course when implemented became the globally reaching Victory Christian Center of Tulsa; Rev. Clarence Boyd, former dean and current Vice President, who pastored generations of ORU students; Rev. John Samuel of Oklahoma City; Rev. John Daniel of Orlando; Rev. Ted Estes, a fellow chaplain from the City of Faith and a beloved pastor in Claremore, Oklahoma; Rev. Tom John of Church of All Nations in Tulsa; Rev. Barry Simon of The Assembly in Broken Arrow, Oklahoma; and Rev. William Valmyr of South Florida.

Internationally, I must mention Pastors Lia Chan and How Tan of Singapore who discovered the key to developing a mega youth church, Pastor Bugvi Olsen who represents whole person ministry in the Faroe Islands, and the many pastors in Mavelikara West district of IPC where I was given the honorary title, District Patron, when my father passed away and my younger brother John replaced him as District Pastor.

This list does not include my siblings who are all in ministry—Dr. and Mrs. John K. Mathew, Rev. and Mrs. K. M. Thimothy, Rev. and Mrs. Oonnoonni Mathew, Rev. and Mrs. G. Samuel, Rev. and Mrs. Johnson Samuel, and Rev. and Mrs. George K. Stephenson (Molly's brother who pastors the International Pentecostal Assembly of God in Chicago).

## Saying Thank You After 37 Years

I received a letter from a special person in New York City. In fact, it was the reply to a note I had sent her. I have seen this woman named Cathy (not her real name) only once. It was in 1972, in the sky!

September 8, 1972! The day I arrived in the United States! A young fellow with little travel experience, with big dreams and bigger apprehensions, I had begun my journey to Yale University in New Haven, Connecticut, from Cochin airport in southwestern India on September 7th.

After a night in Bombay and a couple of stops in the Middle East, I arrived in London. I left London on a British Airways (then known as BOAC) flight to New York. Seated next to me on that flight were two Black females—one young woman and the other who could have been her mother.

I had sent a letter to my relative in New York (John Varghese) before leaving India, informing him of my arrival, but was not sure that he had received my message. The thought of arriving at John F. Kennedy Airport without anyone meeting me there was frightening. I had the ticket to continue my journey from New York to the tiny airport in New Haven but had no idea how to make the transfer in New York. My mind was filled with petrifying thoughts about being stranded in New York with only $8 in my pocket.

My fear must have been visible. The women sitting next to me inquired about my situation. I told them my dilemma. They told me that they were Christians and New Yorkers, and that if I needed any help at JFK, they would assist me. Their kind words gave me much comfort. As we were landing in New York, they wrote their addresses and phone numbers in a notebook I had in my hand, and said, "Not only today, but as long as you are in the United States, if you run into any need, don't hesitate to call us. We will help you." [Can you imagine this happening in the 21$^{st}$ century?]

As we came out through immigration at JFK airport, I was relieved to find my relative waiting for me with several friends with him. So, the ladies said goodbye and went on their way. I have never seen them since.

After 37 years, I came across the old notebook and noticed in it the addresses and phone numbers written in very unfamiliar handwritings. I realized that I had never called them for any help. I also realized that I had never said a thank you to them for their kindness to me.

Where would you find them after all these years? Who knows what these women's names might be now? I tried to forget the whole thing, but a need to say thank you lingered.

# A Seminary Dean's Experiment with Servant Leadership

Molly joined me in my search for these women from my past. The phone numbers they supplied proved useless, so we decided to use the internet which yielded one of the two names and two addresses. We had no idea if we had the right person, but I decided to write a letter of introduction and gratitude and mailed a copy to each address.

The letter I sent to Florida came back stamped, Addressee Unknown. The response from New York City came in a big envelope with the following information.

Cathy was the younger of the two women. Her senior companion was her mother's friend and her mentor. They were in London visiting Cathy's relatives there and were on their way back on that flight in 1972. Her mentor has died.

Cathy never married, so her name never changed! She took care of her disabled parents until they passed away. Her mother died first. Three years later, she lost her father too. Soon after, she was diagnosed with cancer, but was in remission for a while. She still finds time to help the needy in her community.

It appears that my thank you note lifted Cathy's spirit. I do not know if she ever wondered what happened to the preacher's kid she met in the sky, but I am well aware of the blessings I have received in America. And, of my indebtedness to many: Parents. Teachers. Spouse. Friends. Bosses. Colleagues. Cathy. Mrs. Livingstone. And many others.

Above all, to God our Father from whom all blessings flow!

Thomson K. Mathew

## A Heartfelt Thank You to a Powerful Team

As the dean, I had a very capable administrative team. I believed in over-communication which prevented gossip and suspicion within our group. I trusted every member of the team and shared with them as much information as I could, especially during institutional crisis times. I did the same with the faculty. We had open faculty meetings where members could express any of their feelings and there was a covenant among us to keep relevant matters confidential. We also had really moving spiritual experiences in the faculty plenary sessions at the beginning and end of each semester, and even during our regular faculty meetings as I included a time of prayer and devotion on the agenda each time. God moved in special ways on many occasions.

The administrative team consisted of the dean, associate dean, director of the DMin program, director of field education and assessment, director of the distance education program, and the dean of students. I was fortunate to have some of God's best servants representing these areas throughout my tenure. Their commitment to the mission of the seminary and their sacrificial labors with the faculty and staff made the ORU Seminary a spiritually alive academic institution. Laughter of students filled the hallways. Dr. Mayton's humming of hymns could be heard in our offices as he passed by. Students could be seen going into the seminary chapel for prayer and meditation. With gratitude I remember the people who led this place: Dr. Cheryl Iverson, Dr. Kenneth Mayton, Dr. John Thompson, Dr. James Norwood, Dr. James Barber, Dr. Lillian Breckenridge, and Dr. Tim Ekblad. Dr.

## A Seminary Dean's Experiment with Servant Leadership

Lillian Breckenridge passed away. I still hear from all others from time to time, including Dr. Lillian's husband Dr. James Breckenridge, who is still teaching in the seminary.

Judy Cope was most helpful to me as my administrative assistant. She had come to ORU campus from Alabama first to enroll her daughter Amy as a student and based on her experiences on campus felt that ORU could use her services. Her husband Ken Cope and she moved to Tulsa by faith and started looking for a position at ORU. She became part of our team.

Later the Copes became our neighbors in Jenks. Mr. Ken Cope, a professional woodworker, was a gentle person who helped Molly by volunteering to transport her to work during heavy snow days. The Copes were good neighbors who helped us in many ways and our kids are fond of them. At one time when Jamie was home alone during one of our trips, she was shocked to see a snake in our living room; Mr. Cope responded instantly to her frantic call, came to the house, and caught the snake using one of his woodworking tools. Jamie has been grateful to him for helping her while we were away. She has written up this story in gratitude.

Another person with a significant impact on me and the seminary was Dr. Cheryl Iverson. Iverson was a Pentecostal pastor as a young woman in Canada, where she was raised, and came to ORU in the early 1980s for graduate study in theology. She has a very moving testimony regarding how God made her study at ORU possible through a faithful supporter who was committed to helping her fulfill God's call on her life. Encouraged by Dean Chappell, she went to his alma mater,

Drew University in New Jersey, following her graduation from ORU and completed a PhD in Old Testament studies. She returned as a professor in the undergraduate department of theology while Dr. Chappell was still dean. She later became the chair of the department.

Even though I knew Dr. Iverson, my first encounter with her was after I became the associate dean under Dr. Horner. At that time Dr. Ervin, the most senior professor in the seminary, was retiring maybe for the second or third time. I approached Dr. Iverson to inquire about the possibility of her becoming the professor of Old Testament in the graduate school, leaving her chairmanship in the undergraduate department. It never really took place but when I became dean, I went back to her and requested she consider becoming the associate dean. She agreed and moved to the academic office in the seminary in 2000. She has been an outstanding dean for academic affairs and served students and teachers very faithfully, and remained a loyal friend, associate, and prayer partner in our lives. Her help and support made the school a stronger institution. As a person who pays attention to details, she preserved important documents, kept exceptionally good records, and put academic processes and procedures in place to assist faculty and students. Her husband Randy Iverson has been a strong supporter of her work at ORU. They remain close friends and prayer partners to us now.

When Dr. Iverson and I used to attend various ATS conferences at the beginning of our leadership at ORU, we had conversations with deans from mainline seminaries that gave us the impression that we were seen as participants from the margins of Christianity, although we represented a seminary from the largest and fastest growing segment of global Christianity. However, through the years ATS leaders recognized our leadership and knowledge of academic standards and learned of the academic reputation of our seminary and began to involve us in the association in different ways. Dr. Iverson was selected to be a mentor in the women in leadership efforts of ATS and I was asked not only to join several accreditation site visit teams but also to lead such teams to major mainline Protestant seminaries in the United States. We developed personal relationships with a number of ATS officials which proved to be a great blessing to ORU, and to us personally. Dr. Lester Ruiz is one of them who became a friend to me. I believe Dr. Dan Alshire's long-term leadership at the ATS made it a better organization.

## Thanks, Iverson

I am grateful to Dr. Iverson for her hard work and particularly for her character. There were times when we had challenges with employees and students where she was an immensely helpful ally to me as she kept meticulous documentation of events which helped us during several difficult situations. At one time a student wrote a very hurtful letter concerning me to the new president, Dr. Wilson, who really did not know my style of leadership at that time, although he knew of my reputation. Finding out what happened, Dr. Iverson met with all the administrators of the seminary and drafted a letter to the president stating the facts of the situation and showing how the student was not telling the truth. Even though I had not asked her to write a letter to Dr. Wilson on my behalf to clear my name, I am grateful for her kindness, along with the support of the seminary administrators.

On another occasion, a person was upset with me, claiming that I did not discipline another employee who used profanity in the hallway. I did not even know about the situation and in our meeting with this individual, Dr. Iverson helped the upset person to see the facts of the situation. There was another time a student began to speak to me in a disrespectful manner in a meeting where the student was called in to address a disciplinary matter. Dr. Iverson pointed out the student's attitude, counseled him regarding the need to respect authority, and ended the meeting. For all the problematic meetings with staff and disciplinary meetings with students, I have always had Dr. Iverson join me as a participant and witness, and especially when I met with females. When she was not available, I had Judy Cope join me when I met with female students. On many occasions, when I prepared for difficult challenges administratively or otherwise, I asked available team members to join me for prayer.

*Part III*

# Lessons

*Chapter 9*

# Lessons on Ministry, Leadership, and Life

## Seven Things I Wish All Leaders Knew

Having been an academic leader, minister of the Gospel, and a confidant to many leaders of major ministries and mega churches, I wish all leaders knew the following lessons. I learned these by watching religious institutions, high-profile leaders, and by being with people during difficult times. Watching some of them was like seeing an accident in slow motion. I wish I knew how to convince emerging leaders how important the following simple truths are.

1. Power, Influence, and *Illusion* of Power Are Not the Same
   Leaders should know the difference between power, influence, and the *illusion* of power. Rank or title-based power is the lowest level of power. Influence is the highest level

of power one can have. Rank matters, but in non-profit organizations with the mission to make a difference in people's lives, influence through inspiration and example is the best form of power. Any leader can be deceived with an illusion of power. I have seen leaders exercise excessive power and realize much too late that what they perceived to have had was not real power but only an illusion of power that was wrongly reinforced by those surrounding them who did so only to benefit themselves.

2. Learn the Power of Powerlessness

    The Power of powerlessness simply represents the power of one's character and/or moral standing in an organization. Having a reputation of integrity in an organization and the willingness to ignore personal fears to speak up at the right moments are the only requirements needed to exercise this power. As a mid-level leader in a large organization, I have had several opportunities to exercise this power. Most of the time it had to do with speaking up for those who were not in a position to speak. I have been in meetings and situations as the lowest ranked person present, where decisions made there could negatively impact people who were not at the table. I was certainly tempted not to stick my neck out and risk my good standing with the people involved. However, more than once, I was able to speak the truth in love based purely on my personal standing and witness in the organization. Leaders who did not expect my spoken comments when given have expressed their appreciation for my words after the fact more than once.

## A Seminary Dean's Experiment with Servant Leadership

3. Balance in Life is a Necessity

   Leadership can be all-consuming. American style of leadership in non-profit organizations can send the leader to burnout and even the hospital, if not careful. It is easy to neglect one's life and lose the equilibrium of life. Richard Exley wrote long ago that Christian leaders should have a rhythm of life which should balance work, worship, rest, and play.[1] My experience is that it is easier said than done in the business of saving the world. I have not always practiced what I am preaching here and have suffered because of it, even though I have really tried. The truth is that no one is indispensable. In Christian theology, you only need to be willing to die for your faith, you do not have to commit suicide. Perfectionism has a high price and feeling that it is better to do all things personally than to accept less than perfect work products from associates is really foolishness. I know this better now as a former dean than I did when I was a dean. I trust my readers will learn from my mistakes.

4. Kingdom Building Requires Kingdom Values

   The church and seminary are in the same business. It is the business of expanding the boundaries of the kingdom of God in the world. I have seen some sincere Christian leaders using values that are contradictory to the values of the kingdom of God to *expand* the kingdom of God, but ultimately failing miserably. The values of the kingdom of God are upside down. Christianity is ultimately

---

[1] Richard Exley, *The Rhythm of Life* (Colorado Springs, CO: David C. Cook, 1987.)

countercultural. Building a Christian organization using unchristian principles is not a workable plan. Structures built with hay and stubble have a way of burning out without much residue. Unfortunately, the undoing of such building takes some time, but the damage caused is significant and long lasting.

5. Build People, Not Things

   Do not use people to build things, instead, use things (resources) to build people. I have noticed that when leaders use people in an abusive way to build things, they lose both people and things at the end. Those who build up people by using the things (resources) at their disposal seem to retain both people and things in a lasting way.

6. There is a Difference Between Vision and Midlife Crisis

   It is natural to seek significance in midlife, but it should not be at the expense of helpless associates. I have seen leaders investing energy and resources in unnecessary projects and destroying a lot of innocent people in the process of doing so. It may be appropriate for some boards to consider these questions before approving major projects: Is this project a visionary effort or a monument to self? Is our leader having a midlife crisis? It is not uncommon for Christian leaders to be tempted to build their own kingdoms, but ministry's goal is to build God's kingdom, not our own.

7. Don't Be Proud of Giving Headaches

   I was in a meeting once with a Christian leader when he was told about the headaches (distress) of his followers who were trying to fulfill the unreasonable demands he had placed on them. I will never forget his response. He said, "I don't have headaches. I give headaches!" This is not a good attitude for any leader. Remembering that the values of the kingdom of God are countercultural has helped me to deal with my associates, staff, and students in a kinder way. In God's kingdom, giving is the way to receive, dying is the way to live, and serving is the way to lead!

## Ten Life Lessons

As required by the accrediting association, seminary students at ORU undergo a formal assessment process. Most go through an intentionally designed three-step process. The final step is a professional assessment to determine the students' readiness for ministry as they approach graduation. The dean gets to address each cohort of students concerning their ministerial development and formation on several occasions during their studies. During an institutional crisis, I shared with the students these life lessons:

1. A leader must overcommunicate, especially during crises, because a void of information produces super-sized gossips.
2. A crisis moment can bring unlikely leaders to power but also unusual opportunities for the future.
3. A leadership team must practice confidentiality. Lack of confidentiality causes the death of confidence in the team.
4. No one in an organization, no matter how important their role may seem, is indispensable.

5. We must keep the matter of our salvation a priority. God has no grandchildren. We must work out our own salvation. That means, we should not let our work for the Lord send us to hell.
6. You must discover your own identity and purpose. Others can help you in this process, but they cannot own it for you.
7. All of us have unwholesome elements of our past that influence us now, often unconsciously. We are tempted to hide these elements or deny them. Owning the past will help you to redeem the past, by the grace of God and through the power of the Holy Spirit.
8. The business aspects of ministry cannot be ignored. It does not take care of itself. Pay attention to this like your future depends on it. You can do good ministry and gain much accomplished, but if you ignored the business aspect, it would hurt you later. There is a difference between business and business-like. Run your ministry in a business-like fashion.
9. Unattended issues of life can catch up with you and ruin your life and ministry. Pay attention and seek help. Remain open to receive help. Repent and confess when needed. Apologize when it is the right thing to do.
10. Recognize the people who make you successful or look good. Share credit and the benefits with them.

## Stay With the Call

Despite the widespread misunderstanding about Christian ministry, ordained ministers are not the only ministers of the

## A Seminary Dean's Experiment with Servant Leadership

gospel. God gave the apostles, prophets, evangelists, pastors, and teachers for the equipping of the saints to do the work of the ministry, according to Ephesians 4:12. To a large degree, ministry is simply equipping and enabling disciples of Jesus to fulfill the multiple ministries of God's church. The ultimate purpose of the ordained ministry is, therefore, to produce people who minister. Although not all are called to the offices of ministry, all believers are called to serve. The true purpose of ministry is to produce ministers by enabling the followers of Jesus to serve others in the name of Jesus, by edifying, building, equipping, and helping them to grow.

Not all ministers are serving in local congregations or denominational headquarters. I was called to prepare people for the work of the ministry through seminary education. I never doubted that sense of calling to prepare people for professional Christian ministry, even when people introduced me at conventions as if I had a secular job. I was a pastor-leader of a theological seminary where we were trying to help people receive training that matched their calling.

On two occasions during my tenure as dean I was considered for the position of provost, the chief academic officer of the university. It was a serious consideration on the second occasion because key leaders were involved in it. I had an exceptionally good professional and personal relationship with each provost I served. I had worked with them in confronting several thorny issues through the years related to personnel, accreditation, etc. Molly and I were returning from a trip to the Silver Dollar City area when I received the call on the second occasion with the proposal to train me to become the next provost. I was flattered and told the caller that we would consider the kind offer. Certainly, a higher salary and indoor parking looked attractive to me!

We prayed about this proposal, but one question kept coming up—Has the Lord called us to train people for Christian ministry at ORU Seminary, working with a world-class faculty, or to become the university's provost who must worry about academic matters in all the colleges? There is nothing wrong with a person becoming a university provost if the individual involved has a calling to do that type of important work that has a wide range of responsibilities. I did not have such a call and so the answer was obvious. We called back and declined the offer, and never regretted that decision. Even though the single-minded response to God's call to serve as dean of the College of Theology and Ministry at ORU was hard work that affected our whole family profoundly, we have the peace-giving assurance that we were following and fulfilling God's call on our lives. [I was able to live below my means with my salary as dean and the walk to the office from the executive parking lot was really not bad.]

Functioning outside one's call is not a good thing. I know a saintly man who had a recognized ministry of speaking pastorally into people's lives with real discernment. Dr. Kenneth Mayton and I joined him on several occasions when he prayed for individuals whom we knew well but he did not. At times, Dr. Mayton and I looked at each other in disbelief in the middle of some prayers due to the accuracy of his discernment about the people he was praying for. Eventually, because of his good pastoral work, he was offered

## A Seminary Dean's Experiment with Servant Leadership

a position of authority in an area where he lacked qualifications and skills. He accepted it and began to function in that position in good faith, but due to being outside his calling and preparation, he caused much distress to the people who offered him that position and to those people who needed his authentic ministry.

His ministry became counterproductive, and he had to leave the organization abruptly. I think of him when I think of people who wander outside their area of calling. Even when a position seems attractive or lucrative, one must make sure that it fits one's calling. We excel when our training matches our calling, and we stay within that calling. I wish more Christian leaders knew this truth.

Being drawn by a higher pay or better perks of a new job is natural, but they are not always indications of God's call or confirmation of God's will. Discover your calling first and seek to follow it to the best of your ability. Following your calling does not guarantee a trouble-free life. Christian leaders must accept this truth and prepare their loved ones to prevent them from being disillusioned.

I had asked Molly a difficult question before she said "I do" at our wedding ceremony. I asked, "I am choosing to follow God's call to be a minister. Based on all I know now and as both of us know from our parents' lives, this life may have many hardships. Are you willing to face them with me no matter how hard it gets?" She answered "yes" without any hesitation. She has kept her promise throughout our life together, but thankfully we never had to deal with the kind of situations I had feared. God has been faithful, and He has blessed us spiritually and materially, way beyond anything we could have asked. Thanks be to God!

## Skip the Long Road to Hell

One would not expect it but there are times when morally wrong options are brought to a seminary dean. Even in a Christian institution, proposals can come to leaders from self-interested people to violate their principles or to take unethical shortcuts. Resist such temptations with everything you have in you. Once I had to respond to such a proposal with these words: "I could take a short-cut to hell from India. I didn't do it. Why should I take the long road to hell from the USA?"

Some such proposers will not give up easily. Once a person wanted me to require all students in the college to buy a certain optional academic product at an unreasonably high price to profit him. He offered me a kick-back. When I resisted, he called some ORU board members and told them that I was hindering him from making a significant contribution to the university. He never told them the full story, and this was during a financially difficult time at the university. Fortunately, I had ethical bosses who trusted me. I was able to give them the missing information and they supported my decision.

## Butcher or Neurosurgeon?

In the Pentecostal/charismatic community, there is widespread misunderstanding about theological higher education. Because the anointing of the Holy Spirit is emphasized and the work of the Holy Spirit is given priority, there are some who sincerely believe that no human preparation is required to be effective in ministry. As a result, some call seminaries cemeteries. Others declare with pride that they are not trained in a seminary but in the school of the Holy Spirit. Still others say they did not study theology but were schooled in knee-ology. Many have asked me why they needed a seminary education. To some of these I have asked if Jesus required his disciples to receive three and a half years of training in a primitive world, how much more would He require in our postmodern world? I also had to remind some that training for ministry itself was ministry. Jesus' disciples never graduated! Their professor died, rose again, and physically left them.

Another example I have used is the difference between a butcher and a neurosurgeon. I pointed out that both the butcher and neurosurgeon use knives with two outcomes, one producing meat and the other bringing out healing. I have compared the knife to the Bible, the sword of the Spirit, and said that the way they handled the Bible made a difference. I pointed out that there are butcher-pastors and neurosurgeon-pastors, depending on the way they use the Bible. I have convinced many, especially some mega church pastors who lacked formal theological education, to enroll in seminary and train themselves for a more excellent ministry. I challenged potential students by saying that there is always a more excellent way to minister. We must seek excellence in ministry.

## Don't Guard the Ditch

I had a very capable leader in the church in New Haven who had a sudden change in attitude toward me and the church. This was a gifted person who was involved in important ministries in the church and served on several committees. Initially I thought the change was due to the stress of being overactive in the life of the church. I approached the person with my concern and offered to be helpful in any way, but the person was not responsive, instead took certain actions that were personally painful to me.

I shared my concern with the leadership team and sought counsel. They were sympathetic but not able to offer a solution. Having failed to improve the situation, I decided to go on with my life and ministry. I had some pain and was mystified because what the individual was doing did not make any sense. When I left the church and moved on to the next chapter of my life, the question of why this former ally caused personal pain remained unsolved, but I decided to release the matter to God.

Three decades went by and one day I received a letter in my office from someone whose handwriting I did not recognize. The letter was from the old ally and the message in it was clear. It said, "I have felt impressed in the last few months to write you to express my sorrow for having caused you pain as a young pastor. Please forgive me. Heb 13:17." I accepted the apology and sent a response expressing my love and best wishes.

I learned an important lesson. Sometimes unexplainable things happen in ministry and leadership. Some people who cause pain may not even know why they do so. We must resist the temptation to be bitter about those experiences. It is better to keep in mind that God continues to work in His children's lives even when they displease Him. He is full of mercy and grace and provides all His children opportunities to repent and make things right. While God works on us to transform us into the image of His son, we must not entertain hurt and bitterness toward each other.

Bitterness is our way of keeping people who cause us pain in an emotional ditch in our hearts. The problem is that no one remains in a ditch voluntarily which causes us to guard the ditch. This prevents us from moving forward in our journey of faith. In fact, the offender may advance in his journey of faith while we guard an empty ditch. My advice to leaders who experience friendly fire or unexplainable pain is simple: Move on. Do not waste your life guarding a ditch.

## Mission, Mission, Mission

I am convinced that success in leadership in any organization is directly proportional to its leader's ability to stay focused on the mission of the organization and the ability to keep the followers in line with that mission. Oral Roberts was so focused on the mission of the university that he began almost all consequential meetings with key leaders and the faculty with a review of the university's history and its reason for existing. As a young employee, I used to wonder why he was repeating himself so often. I understand the reason better now.

The founding vision of the university emerged out of Oral's obedience to God's mandate to build a university on God's authority and on the Holy Spirit. He was commissioned to "Raise up your students to hear My voice, to go where

My light is dim, where My voice is heard small, and My healing power is not known, even to the uttermost bounds of the earth. Their work will exceed yours, and in this I am well pleased." It was not an accident that he had the vision statement of the university inscribed on the balcony wall of the chapel. I do not know how many times we were asked to turn around in chapel and read this statement in unison. He wanted to make sure that everyone in the community knew why we were there. No wonder, most graduates can recite ORU's vision statement from memory even decades after their graduation.

ORU's mission statement was clear: "The mission of Oral Roberts University is to develop Spirit-empowered leaders through whole person education to impact the world with God's healing." The idea was that "lawyers are healers too." All the provosts under whom I served—Drs. Carl Hamilton, Ralph Fagin, Mark Lewandowski, Debbie Sowell, and Kathleen Reid-Martinez—were very mindful of the mission statement.

During my deanship, every decision regarding the degree programs and the hiring of faculty and staff was based on the mission. As mentioned above, the faculty examined every course in the seminary in light of the vision and mission of the university, purpose of the seminary, and the objectives of each degree. This type of purposeful commitment to the mission produced the outstanding graduates of our school. Christian leaders should pay close attention to the mission of their organizations and resist making major decisions based on random factors.

A Seminary Dean's Experiment with Servant Leadership

## Leading is Caring

As a professor of pastoral care, I believe that Christian organizations would benefit if they defined the word leading as caring. I begin my Introduction to Pastoral Care course with this strange definition of caring: caring is loving, loving is giving, giving is giving of self, and giving of self is giving of time as the currency of one's life. How do you exercise caring as leading in a multi-layered organization like a university seminary? I believe the model of pastoral care practiced in healthy large churches is the key.

In a healthy large church, the senior pastor is responsible for pastoral care but does not do all the caregiving. The pastor *generally* cares for the whole flock but trains the church in the ministry of caregiving and personally cares for the immediate circle of leaders. Each of them in turn will care for the people under their supervision. Those receiving their care will care for the next level of people. This goes down all the way to the smallest group in the church. Unfortunately, many churches have only so-called "care groups," which are really "didactic" groups led by people untrained in caregiving skills. I made sure that even our weekly administrators' meetings in the seminary were conducted as a care group! That sense of caring went down the whole organization.

I am a believer that you cannot give that which you do not have. I can testify that caring leaders who are focused on institutional mission, unlike leaders who breathe on associates' necks and take pride in giving them headaches, will get the best work out of their staff. And their work will produce great outcomes.

## Ask For Feedback Even When It Hurts

It was my practice to ask for feedback from faculty and students at the end of each semester. We conducted faculty plenary sessions at the beginning and end of each semester where professors and staff met for several sessions to plan the upcoming semester in the beginning and to review the semester at the end. Cancelling the "pot-luck" culture I inherited, I made sure that a good lunch was provided to all attendees each day. Continuing education and orientation to new initiatives were given to the faculty and staff and ideas were discussed and debated in these sessions. [I learned this from Jesus and am grateful to the provosts who understood the need and approved my meal requests.] Judy Cope was a gifted planner of meals and a gracious hostess. Our mealtimes were refreshing to all of us. We also had powerful spiritual moments during many of the plenary sessions.

The seminary administrators reviewed the feedback from the year-end plenary sessions during the summer and made necessary changes based on the input. I created a retreat-type event for administrators and staff to evaluate their areas and to consider the feedback received from the plenaries.

I also met with every graduating class and asked the students to give me an appraisal of their experience as students in the seminary. I asked for feedback on our teaching, administration, facilities, campus life, etc. I promised the students that they could say whatever they wished without worrying about any negative responses from me or anyone else in the seminary. Normally, the dean's office did not get much negative feedback, out of respect or because we were serving them well, or they did not believe my promise of no repercussions. Some of the complaints were regarding the big university systems with which seminary students had to deal with regarding financial and other matters. This was understandable because the university systems were designed with the residential undergraduate students in mind until recently.

It was difficult at times to hear honest student feedback and it was even more so when some students took advantage of the opportunity to give me an earful of bitter grievances about faculty, staff, administrators, or academic procedures without taking any personal responsibility. Sometimes I felt like walking out but chose to stay. At times, it was so hard to hear the negative comments that I had to ask students to say what they wished in a way that I could hear them without being too defensive on behalf of the faculty, staff, or administrators. I had a staff person taking detailed notes on the feedback and we went over the student concerns with administrators and faculty later. Many changes were made as a result of this process to improve the quality of our programs and services.

I used to meet with the senior classes of undergraduates also to hear their concerns and to give them a final pep talk. The undergraduates were kinder and gentler! I highly recommend department chairs and deans of colleges to take this approach despite the pain and discomfort involved. ORU College of Theology and Ministry became a better place because of my willingness to accept the discomfort.

## Don't Take Your Assessment Too Seriously

I was blessed to visit Rev. Yonggi Cho at his residence during my visits to Korea. When I was with Dr. Vinson Synan during the second visit, we had a private dinner with Rev. Cho. He told many stories during that dinner. Dr. Synan asked him many questions about the state of the church in Korea. In response to the question, "How is the Assemblies of God doing in Korea?" Dr. Cho laughingly replied, "I am the Assemblies of God in Korea."

A memorable story I heard that night was about the Pentecostal Holiness Church, Dr. Synan's denomination where his father was bishop at one time, which denied young Yonggi Cho's application for ordination, assessing that he lacked the qualities required to be a good pastor. Dr. Synan apologized on behalf of his church and reminded Dr. Cho, the founding pastor of the largest church in the world, that it was not his first apology for the bad assessment.

Seminaries assess students for readiness for ordination and ministry. This is important work, but sometimes we forget the types of people Jesus chose to be his disciples, and officially pronounce some of our students unqualified for ministry, as if we have the last word on this matter. Although faculty and administrators are experienced in this important work, it is a good idea to do such assessment with much humility.

## Wait for Consensus

It was my habit not to rush major decisions through if at all possible. When changes had to be made in policies, procedures, or curriculum, I made sure that the faculty knew the details of the situation or proposals and the reasons for considering them. I allowed ample discussions, including strong dissent. At times it was painful to wait due to deadlines, accreditation standards, or pressure from superiors. Some of my colleagues who had strong convictions about academic quality and integrity were very good at filibustering. I allowed it to take place. I was not always able to give them everything they wanted but did all I could to reach consensus. Sometimes it was just impossible, but I cannot think of one major change that was made in the College of Theology and Ministry without the consensus of the faculty or without receiving the input of other stakeholders when it was warranted, especially those whose workload would be affected by the change. The trust level we had established in the school made such transactions possible.

## Fight for Your Team

There were times when decisions were made or directions were given by my supervisors, often for good reasons and in good faith, that were going to affect my team of faculty and staff negatively. I never said "Amen" at the first time such a decision was made or a specific direction was given. Often the announcement of such decisions was made in the formal deans' meetings. I tried to push back gently in the meetings when I felt that was needed. When I could not get anywhere by doing so, I made multiple trips later to meet with the decision makers to present my case. I worked as if all decisions in the organization were negotiable until I learned that a particular decision was not.

I was fortunate to work under great provosts who trusted my concern and judgment. They accompanied me to the president's office to appeal when that was an option. I always kept the protocol of not bypassing my immediate supervisors. I was given a break by my leaders on many occasions. I used to make so many trips upstairs on a regular basis that students and staff used to joke about the carpet I was wearing out and about the aerobic points I was gaining each day.

I made those trips for single mothers on staff who needed an increase in pay or a sick faculty member who needed a reduction in teaching schedule or a student who encountered an unfortunate situation. Sometimes I did not receive what I sought, but I knew always that I had done all I could to intercede for my team member. Sometimes other deans asked me how I got what I got. I just smiled normally. When I did tell them what my trick was, some did not seem to believe it.

## Practice Stewardship of Relationship

Most Christian leaders know the importance of stewardship regarding time, talent, and treasure. True servant leadership requires more. As a professor of pastoral care, I learned that stewardship of relationship is even more important. I am not only accountable to God for my relationship to my wife, children, and other people closely related to me. I must also give an account to God for my relationship with the lowest person on the power ladder in my organization. I must remember that they are under my care as a leader. We find these words in the Gospel of Matthew concerning the Son of Man and judgment:

"Then He will answer them, saying, 'Assuredly, I say to you, inasmuch as you did not do *it* to one of the least of these, you did not do *it* to Me.' And these will go away into everlasting punishment, but the righteous into eternal life." (Matt 25:45, 46).

I do not think that this instruction is only about charity work. It is the biblical standard for relationship. Unfortunately, I have witnessed this rule being violated by many leaders who were good stewards of time, talent, and treasure. I wondered if they ever thought about their stewardship of relationships.

## Release Women to Lead

I was born in the largest democracy in the world which had a woman—Mrs. Indira Gandhi—as prime minister but my faith group is not known for promoting women's leadership. However, I believe the words of the prophet Joel:

> "And it shall come to pass afterward
> That I will pour out My Spirit on all flesh;
> **Your sons and your daughters shall prophesy**,
> Your old men shall dream dreams,
> Your young men shall see visions"
> 
> (Joel 2:28, emphasis added)

I was always sure that God did not want to lay off fifty percent of His children from His service. I could not think of any other way to think or operate in a Spirit-empowered community. The women leaders Paul the apostle commended in his writings encouraged me to raise two daughters who are strong women of God—a licensed psychologist and an attorney—and trust the leadership of women who were on the ORU faculty and staff. I learned that when opportunities and resources were provided, women excelled in their assignments and produced great outcomes.

Dr. Cheryl Iverson was the only associate dean I had throughout my deanship. Dr. Lillian Breckenridge pioneered our modular and distance education program. Dr. Ann Young was a coworker of Dr. Ed Decker and provided recognized leadership in the MA in Christian Counseling program. Professor Carol Blan was a capable chair in the undergraduate Theology department for several years. Drs. Sandra Richardson, Andrea Walker, and Kelly James made significant contributions to the quality and life of the seminary. Judy Cope gave leadership to the staff in an excellent fashion. Capable women on her team included Gerry Farrow and Celine Butler in the DMin area, Marlene Mankins in the Assessment office, Debra Watkins in the Admissions area, Evelyn Turner in Student Affairs, Mary Kathryn Tyson in the undergraduate office, and through the years many outstanding student workers like Heather F. Wright, a young woman who came from the mission field to study and returned better prepared. These women exemplified unselfish service, hard work, and deep commitment to the mission of the school. I exhort all leaders to review their position on women in leadership and take this opportunity to critically evaluate their organizations' systemic approach to women in leadership.

# A Seminary Dean's Experiment with Servant Leadership

## You Need a Peer Group

The 1980s was a period that witnessed the fall of several high-profile evangelists and religious leaders. Although Oral Roberts had nothing to do with it, this situation affected the Oral Roberts Ministry in different ways. As I examined the cases of the fallen preachers, one thing became very apparent to me: almost all the ministers who fell seemed to believe and act as if they were peerless. Jesus Christ is the only peerless person in all of history. Even the most gifted person should not consider himself peerless.

Because of the CPE training I had, I have always believed in the need for, and power of, a peer group. I was fortunate to have a built-in peer group at the City of Faith. Chaplains needed to celebrate their joys of success in ministry and more often to process challenges in ministry and the multiple dimensions of pain they witnessed. Although the emotional need related to the work was much less acute as a dean, compared to a chaplain, I made the seminary administrative team a trusted peer group. Although we had differences in rank, I did everything I could to create a fearless climate of trust where authentic opinions were invited, and confidentiality was a given.

Prayer was a major component of all our weekly administrative meetings. I received true feedback and experienced the most powerful prayer times during some of these meetings. I witnessed immediate answers to thorny situations after such prayers several times during the mega transitions at the university. Dr. James Norwood led us in some of the most moving prayers. On one occasion, after a desperate prayer led by Dr. Ken Mayton, the team was thankful and surprised to see God solve an almost impossible situation within hours.

I do not know if it was due to my birth order as a firstborn or my CPE experience, I was inclined to develop a team that functioned as a peer group. My peer group was not limited to the administrators. There was a small faculty lunchroom which witnessed the formation of true friendships and an authentic peer group. Some of the best theological ideas and concepts developed at ORU to articulate a Pentecostal/charismatic perspective on life and ministry came out of our lunch time discussions. No one who participated in this will forget the tight seating in the small room where we ate, talked, laughed, and shared ideas and our hearts. In retrospect, I failed to have a peer group during my pastorate in New Haven which made my life and work there more difficult.

I was also fortunate to have a very good seminary advisory committee made up of highly regarded people with extensive knowledge and experience in ministry, scholarship, and theological education. Although having such a committee was a requirement of ATS for university-related seminaries, I truly appreciated their oversight and guidance. They gave me and my team accountability and advocacy. Former Fuller Seminary provost, Dr. Russell Spittler, United Methodist pastor and my DMin classmate, Dr. Tom Harrison, founding dean of ORU Seminary, Dr. Jimmy Buskirk, Dr. Vinson Synan, while he was at Regent University, former ORU Board members, Dr. Glenda Payas and Dr. Mike Rakes, Pastor Sharon Daugherty of Victory Christian Center, and other distinguished leaders served on the advisory committee at different times. Dr. Synan used to flatter me by calling me "dean of deans!" The formal meetings of the advisory committee ended each time with the entire committee laying hands on me and praying for me. Their prayers, affirmation, and advocacy helped me and the seminary.

## When Terminating, Remember, the Funeral Is for the Living

There are situations when working with certain employees, the only option left is dismissal. There are certainly times when the cause of firing is so severe a farewell is unwise and impossible. However, in many cases, especially involving employees much loved by their coworkers, providing an occasion to express appreciation for their service and to allow coworkers to say good-byes is a good idea. I realize that this is difficult and impossible when mass lay-offs take place. However, as a dean and professor of pastoral care, I found that each firing is a death—death of a dream, and death of a potentially great future for the employee and the institution. Every death deserves a funeral and funerals are not for the dead, no matter how many of the deceased persons' favorite songs we sing. They are for the living to find meaning and comfort. The same applies to terminations.

The disappearance of an employee, especially a well-liked worker, without any explanation is a demoralizing event for those left behind. When the released employee was trustworthy and legally it was doable, I provided an opportunity to celebrate the person's contributions and to express good wishes. This avoided unnecessary paranoia among good employees left behind. At one time, I held a secret unofficial farewell luncheon off campus involving all faculty and staff for a beloved employee. I also secretly met with two high profile individuals who left the organization, just to say goodbye. I am convinced that some legal challenges can be thwarted just by having a decent funeral called a farewell party.

I know this is not standard MBA-given protocol but feel that this approach has some merit in a Christian organization. This is one place we can be countercultural. I do not know if my supervisors knew about the secret farewells I held. In any case, I was thankful not to be fired for such actions.

## Use the Power of Speech-making

Contextually appropriate and inspiring speeches have a prominent place in successful leadership. Dr. Mark Rutland describes his leadership as "leading from the pulpit." During my deanship at ORU, there were historically crucial moments when I was in a position to speak or was asked to speak to the campus community. In my case, these occasions provided opportunities to preach in the chapel or other campus auditoriums. This was outside the normal rotation of preaching in the university chapel on a regular basis that was assigned to me for many years. It has been said that preaching is the articulation of the preacher's inner events, but I found that preaching can also be the articulation of crucial events in a particular context from God's perspective. Preaching like this addresses the inner concerns of the people involved in difficult transitional moments.

I have included in the Appendix the outlines of two such sermons that were delivered at crucial times at ORU. The message titled "I Change Not" offered a word of assurance at a time of great changes on campus. The next one, titled "Moses, Joshua, and Who?" was delivered in the chapel service led by President Mark Rutland on the day Dr. Billy Wilson was elected as his successor. It was given while the election of the new president was being held in the board room. The board members were scheduled to join us in chapel to announce their decision, but they did not arrive in chapel due to the longer time that was required to complete the proceedings. I preached the message to the entire campus community and the media that were waiting in the chapel to report on the leadership transition. Dr. Rutland felt that the message I shared was a word from the Lord for that hour and he sent a digital copy of it to all the board members and other friends of ORU.

## Not India, Not Yale, but Commitment to Jesus

I was recognized as a good leader of the College of Theology and Ministry on many occasions. When provosts ranked deans through an evaluation process, I scored higher than other deans during several years. Sometimes, the provosts told newly appointed deans of other colleges to spend some time with me as a long-serving dean to learn my tricks of the trade. Whether I deserved the recognition or not, I was taken out to lunch by newly appointed deans more than once to comply with the encouragement they received from the provosts.

Some of the deans talked to me like my leadership style had some Indian secret and wanted to figure out that secret. They did not seem to know that I know some Indians who are tyrants as leaders. Others thought that my education at

Yale Divinity School gave me some mysterious ability to lead the way I was leading. More than once I had to tell them that although my unique life is an integrated product of my roots in a pastor's home in India and the education I received at Yale and other schools, my real secret was that I really tried to practice a model of servant leadership that was a result of reading the same Bible they were reading. I had the impression that some of my lunch hosts were not too sure!

Of course, I had my share of losses and leadership challenges, but overall, taking the words of Jesus seriously has paid off well for me. Sometimes my ego was not happy with what I had to say or do as a servant leader. Other times servant leadership did not seem to work. But ultimately, I was a good college and seminary dean because of my humble efforts to practice what I preached. Being a professor of pastoral care was also enormously helpful to be a good dean. The essence of pastoral care is listening. The lessons on active listening I read about and practiced in CPE programs and chaplaincy turned out to be a great blessing to me during my deanship. I was able to see myself as a pastor to the team I worked with. Being open to them, being concerned about their well-being, and being vulnerable to them appropriately helped me to serve the school and the Lord better.

## Leadership Development Is Not a Fast Operation

I will present this lesson in the form of a talk I gave to seminary students who were weary of the time it took to complete their educational journey. I presented three case studies from the Bible, as follows, to demonstrate that God takes His time to develop the leaders He wishes to use for strategic purposes.

## Leadership and Time

Text: 1 Samuel 16: 1

Now the LORD said to Samuel, "How long will you mourn for Saul, seeing I have rejected him from reigning over Israel? Fill your horn with oil, and go; I am sending you to Jesse the Bethlehemite. For I have provided Myself a king among his sons.

## Introduction

The best a seminary can offer is a horn which represents biblical knowledge and ministerial skills but not necessarily oil, which represents the anointing of the Holy Spirit. You will have to get your horn filled with oil. Remember that the church is nervous about horns without oil. Faculty and students should keep this in mind. Faculty should not quench the Spirit and students should not expect knowledge alone to flourish their ministries. A Pentecostal/charismatic seminary must demonstrate that academics and spirituality are compatible.

Many of you are eager to go to or get back to your fields of ministry and become great leaders for God. I have a word of caution for you. You need to be patient because some important things God does, like leadership development, take time.

## Bible Message

We value time and like instant things. The Bible speaks about some things that happened instantly. Consider the following passages:

"Let there be light:" there was light, Genesis 1:3 (Light was created instantly.)

And immediately her flow of blood stopped, Luke 8:44 (A bleeding woman was healed instantly.)

Immediately his leprosy was cleansed, Matthew 8:3 (A leper was healed instantly.)

Immediately their eyes received sight, Matthew 20:33 (Blind men were healed instantly.)

Immediately the fever left her, Mark 1: 31 (Peter's mother-in-law was healed instantly.)

Immediately he arose, took up the bed and went out in the presence of them all, so that all were amazed and glorified God, saying, "we never saw anything like this!" Mark 2: 12 (Lame man at the pool was healed instantly.)

Immediately his feet and ankle bones received strength. So he, leaping up, stood and walked and entered the temple with them—walking, leaping and praising God! Acts 3: 7,8 (Lame at the gate called Beautiful was healed instantly.)

Immediately all the doors were opened and everyone's chains were loosed, Acts 16: 26 (Prison doors opened instantly for Paul and Silas.)

## A Seminary Dean's Experiment with Servant Leadership

We prefer this kind of ministry where things happen immediately. It is wonderful to witness and experience such happenings. These things still do happen from time to time, but when it comes to leadership development, God has a very different strategy. God does not create an instant leader. He does not create an instant disciple. He does not create an instant minister. God's leadership development takes time, and the time it takes depends on the task at hand.

The time required to complete your leadership development depends on the problem God is trying to solve through your leadership. That is why you should remember that your training must match your calling.

Have you noticed that larger planes spend a longer time on the runway? You will also notice that they can stay longer in the air without refueling and are able to reach farther with larger loads. Leadership preparation for strategic goals takes longer than most of us want.

Let me share with you three case studies from the Bible, using mostly scripture texts. You will note that strategic leadership development took time and the time required depended on the problem God was trying to solve.

### Case 1

God had a problem: Abuse of Israelites in Egypt.

So the Egyptians made the children of Israel serve with rigor. And they made their lives bitter with hard bondage--in mortar, in brick, and in all manner of service in the field. All their service in which they made them serve was with rigor (Exodus 1:13-14).

God decided to solve the problem by giving birth to a leader named Moses.

And a man of the house of Levi went and took as wife a daughter of Levi. So the woman conceived and bore a son. And when she saw that he was a beautiful child, she hid him three months (Exodus 2:1-2).

Meanwhile, the problem got worse.

Now it happened in the process of time that the king of Egypt died. Then the children of Israel groaned because of the bondage, and they cried out; and their cry came up to God because of the bondage. So God heard their groaning, and God remembered His covenant with Abraham, with Isaac, and with Jacob. And God looked upon the children of Israel, and God acknowledged them (Exodus 2:23-25).

Moses tried to solve the problem prematurely. It did not go well. Years later, he was *prepared* to lead through much hardship and received the commission to solve the problem. God remained patient with Mosses and provided every resource he needed to solve the problem. Moses was finally ready.

Now Moses was tending the flock of Jethro his father-in-law, the priest of Midian. And he led the flock to the back of the desert, and came to Horeb, the mountain of God. And the Angel of the Lord appeared

# A Seminary Dean's Experiment with Servant Leadership

to him in a flame of fire from the midst of a bush. So he looked, and behold, the bush was burning with fire, but the bush was not consumed (Exodus 3:1-2).

The problem of slavery of the Israelites was eventually solved, but God had to develop Moses as a leader and work through the mistakes he made. The day finally came when Moses stretched out his staff and led the people out of the land of bondage.

Leadership development takes time. Be patient as God is preparing you.

## Case 2

God had a leadership problem: Eli the priest lost vision; his sons were wicked leaders.

God decided to solve the problem by developing a new leader named Samuel.

Problem statement:

> And it came to pass at that time, while Eli was lying down in his place, and when his eyes had begun to grow so dim that he could not see (1 Samuel 3:2).

> Now the sons of Eli were corrupt; they did not know the LORD (1 Samuel 2:12).

There was a praying woman who was misunderstood by Pastor Eli first, but he consoled her later and sent her away in peace. Later she showed up with a child named Samuel.

> Then they slaughtered a bull and brought the child to Eli. And she said, "O my lord! As your soul lives,

my lord, I am the woman who stood by you here, praying to the LORD. For this child I prayed, and the LORD has granted me my petition which I asked of Him. Therefore I also have lent him to the LORD; as long as he lives he shall be lent to the LORD." So they worshiped the LORD there (1 Samuel 1:25-28).

Time was needed for Samuel to grow up and *become* the solution.

Leadership development for God's purposes takes time. We must be patient.

## Case 3

Problem: A disobedient leader, King Saul, who had been anointed by Samuel was removed by God.

Samuel grieved. He received God's instruction to fill his horn with oil to anoint David as the next king.

Samuel was the solution to the Eli problem. Now David is the solution to the Saul problem.

Samuel obeyed God and anointed David, but time was still needed to develop David as the new leader to fulfill God's ultimate purposes.

## Conclusion

You are in the making. You may not even know the problem you are called to solve, but your time is coming. Be patient and trust the process.

An encounter with God and His call brought you to where you are now. Gain knowledge, develop skills, and learn to hear God's voice to become a leader after God's own heart.

Meanwhile, be filled with the Holy Spirit. Learn to be led by the Holy Spirit. That is how you become a servant leader for God.

www.thomsonkmathew.com

# Appendix

# Message One: I Change Not

Texts:

Malachi 3:6
"For I am the Lord, I do not change;
Therefore you are not consumed, O sons of Jacob..."

Hebrews 13:8
Jesus Christ is the same yesterday, today, and forever.

## Introduction

We live in a changing world.

Remember the book *Megatrends*?

I remember reading *Megatrends* and wondering if those predictions would come to pass. I now realize that we are living through those predicted trends. The industrial society has become the information society. The physical labor economy has become a service economy. Our big world has become a small world. We live in a complex world today.

We see changes all around. Politics change. Relationships change. Popular fashions change.

Human beings change through infancy, childhood, adolescence, young adulthood, and old age.

Marriage goes through changes.

Technology has drastically changed our life and lifestyles.

We see major changes in our institution.

Amid these changes, where we see everything changing, we begin to live as if everyone is changing, including God.

## Bible Message

To us God is saying through Malachi: "I am the Lord, I change not."

I. What does "I change not" mean?

1. I believe it means God's love does not change. He loves us unconditionally. His love is called "Agape." The Apostle Paul tells us that while we were yet sinners, Christ died for us.

2. God's power does not change. God's creative power that manifested "in the beginning," His sustaining power that manifested in history, and His renewing power that manifests in our world in multiple ways today do not change.

3. The truth of God's word does not change. Its message about sin and salvation remains true. The wages of sin is death, but the gift of God is eternal life through Jesus Christ.

    4. God's promises do not change. All the promises of God in Jesus are yes and amen. God is a promise keeper.

    5. God's Holiness does not change. Isaiah the prophet and John the apostle described the sounds of heaven: "Holy, Holy, Holy." Holiness is God's character. He does not change.

II. Malachi was looking forward to Jesus but was describing the God of Abraham, Isaac, and Jacob who does not change.

God of the Old Testament is known by many names:

> Jehovah = Eternal God
> Elohim = Great God of glory
> El Elion = Most high God
> El Shaddai = All sufficient God
> Adonai = Lord and Master
> Jehovah Jireh = Provider God
> Jehovah Rapha = God our Healer
> Jehovah Nissi = God our Banner
> Jehovah Kadesh = Holy God
> Jehovah Shalom = God of Peace

We have an everlasting God. We have an almighty God. He is unchanging. He remains the same.

The New Testament tells us that the eternal God became man for us in Jesus Christ.

The Bible tells us: "In the beginning was the word… The word became flesh" in Jesus.

The infinite became an infant for us. God became man and lived among us. The creator became a creation for us.

That is why the author of Hebrews says: Jesus Christ is the same yesterday, today and forever.

During the mega changes we are facing locally and globally, remember that our God does not change. He is the same yesterday, today, and forever.

III. There is more good news: The unchanging God can change you and others.

Philosophies cannot transform human beings.

The unchanging God who became flesh in Jesus can transform us.

Ask these witnesses who were transformed:

1. The transformed Samaritan woman who thought she needed water and a husband (John 4:39)

2. The jailer who was transformed and washed the wounds of his prisoners (Acts 16:33)

3. The man at the gate called Beautiful who was healed and changed (Acts 3:8)

4. The man who climbed a tree to see Jesus, Zacchaeus, who changed (Luke 19:8)

5. The dead man Lazarus who came alive (John 11:44)

IV. The unchanging God can change your situation.

Ask these witnesses whose situations changed:

1. Daniel: The cruel decree changed in his favor (Daniel 6:25-27).
2. Joseph: His brothers were reconciled (Genesis 45:8).
3. Esther: Mordecai did not die despite Haman's efforts and the Israelites were saved (Esther 6:12).
4. Naaman's leprosy was healed (2 Kings 5:14).
5. The lame man at the pool did not die at the pool side. He took up his bed and walked (John 5:8).

## Conclusion

Do you know an individual needing change? Do you need a change in your life? Ask God to change you.

Do you have a situation needing change? Ask God to change your situation for the better.

We have a fast-changing situation at our institution. Do not be afraid. We have a God who does not change. Let us hold on to His steady hand!

Our God is with us in the challenges we face. Our unchanging God can change us and our situation. Let us trust Him and depend on Him.

# Message Two: Moses, Joshua, and Who?

Texts:

Judges 2: 8-10

Now Joshua the son of Nun, the servant of the Lord, died when he was one hundred and ten years old. And they buried him within the border of his inheritance at Timnath Heres, in the mountains of Ephraim, on the north side of Mount Gaash. When all that generation had been gathered to their fathers, another generation arose after them who did not know the Lord nor the work which He had done for Israel.

1 Samuel 8:19

Nevertheless, the people refused to obey the voice of Samuel; and they said, "No, but we will have a king over us…"

## Introduction

I. In the texts, we can discern 4 stages in the history of the people of God.

Stage 1: Moses is the leader of the first generation.

Stage 2: Joshua is the leader of the second generation.

Stage 3: A third generation did not know the Lord.

Stage 4: A fourth generation says that it wants to be like other nations.

## Bible Message

II. Let us examine these stages.

**Stage 1:** Moses is the leader in stage one.

Moses knew God, he heard God, and he was a pioneer.

Moses was a one-of-a-kind leader who accomplished great things.

He made mistakes and did not reach the promised land, but God showed him the land.

He died at the age of 120 and God buried him.

**Stage 2:** Joshua is the leader in stage two.

Moses, the first leader, laid hands on him.

Joshua provided outstanding leadership.

He won several battles and gained new territories. He was greatly respected by the people. We learn that Israel served the Lord all the days of Joshua (Joshua 24: 31).

He died at the age of 110 and was buried in Mount Ephraim.

**Stage 3:** Here we read about a new generation that did not know the Lord and what He had done for Israel.

This is incredible when you look at the history of this people.

The people of Israel began their journey from Egypt with Moses. They had seen God's work, witnessed the plagues, experienced the Passover, and lived through the Red Sea miracle. They sang and danced on the other side of the sea. They ate the manna God provided and drank supernaturally supplied water. They had witnessed the presence of God as a pillar of cloud during the day and as a pillar of fire at night. They were eyewitnesses of God's majesty. Finally, they crossed Jordan and reached the land of promise.

But after Joshua's death, a new generation came that did not know God.

III. How could this happen?

I believe that we need to look at the nature of the generation/s that raised this generation and learn some lessons.

We can see several issues with the parental generation/s in this examination.

1. They had trouble trusting God.

2. They had trouble thanking God.

3. They feared local people.

4. They obviously did not pass down their history and faith to the new generation in a way that they could know it and own it. (The fourth reason is of great interest to me as an educator in a Christian university.)

IV. I believe that God had given the Israelites ancient "PowerPoints" to teach their children. We see these "PowerPoints" in the book of Joshua in the form of stone memorials. The book of Joshua tells the story of three important places with stone memorials.

1. Gilgal had the 12 stones posted in memory of the crossing of Jordan River. The Israelites were instructed to tell their children about the meaning of those stones, that the miracle-working God was their provider (Joshua 4:4).

2. The Valley of Achor had a stone memorial that was to remind them about the punishment of Achan who was stoned there for lying about his sinful actions. They were to teach their children about God's holiness and justice from this "PowerPoint" (Joshua 7: 22-26). God is love. He is also Holy!

3. Shechem had a memorial with one stone where Joshua and the people made the covenant with God after he challenged them to choose whom

they would serve. He testified, "But as for me and my house, we will serve the Lord." (Joshua 24:15).

One generation was supposed to tell their story to their children to teach these lessons:

1. God is the Provider. He is a God of Miracles.

2. God is Holy.

3. Israel is God's people of covenant.

V. Look what happens in Stage 4.

**Stage 4:** This is the generation that wants to be like other nations. We must learn from the history of Israel and tell the story of ORU to the new generation of students. We must tell it in the vocabulary of the current generation so that they will not miss it. Otherwise, we may raise a generation that does not know who they are, where they came from, and God's purposes for their lives. In that case, the generation that follows them will say, like Israel, "We want to be like other nations" (1 Samuel 8:19).

There is nothing wrong about being like other universities in terms of high academic standards, strong faculty, sufficient finances, and excellent facilities. But when it comes to the mission, our purpose of existence, we cannot be like other universities. We should not be like other universities.

We have a powerful calling. We have a unique mission: "To develop Spirit-empowered leaders through whole person education to impact the world with God's healing."

## Conclusion

We must trust God.

We must thank God.

We must not fear local people.

And we must tell our story and teach the important lessons God has taught us.

Our mission cannot be done with human efforts alone. We need the presence and power of the Holy Spirit to accomplish this. We need a true Pentecost. Not as a denomination, but as an encounter and experience.

True Pentecost is the presence of God with the people of God!

[The following is the transcribed text of the valedictorian speech my daughter Elizabeth Susan Mathew (Elizabeth Mathew Koshy, PhD) gave to the class of 2000.]

# Who Wants to Be a Messenger?

Who wants to be a millionaire? In the dawn of a millennium, this is the one question that Americans dream of being asked. However, as society seeks the glamour of fortune and fame, I am reminded of the words found in the Book of Isaiah, Chapter six, verse eight, "Then I heard the voice of the Lord saying, whom shall I send and who will go for us?" Therefore, graduates of Oral Roberts University, there is one simple question placed before us today, to the class of 2000, in a new century, in a new millennium: Who wants to be a messenger, a messenger for God?

Upon entrance into ORU, we each received three lifelines to assist us in our journey of faith. The first lifeline has been our families. Our families have emotionally supported us, have prayed for us, and in some cases, have financed us through our academic pursuits. We would not have made it this far without our families. So we salute you parents, siblings, spouses, children, grandparents, and all other extended family members who have sacrificed your lives for us. And yet with this lifeline, the question still resounds: Who wants to be a messenger, a messenger for God?

Our second lifeline here at ORU has been our friends. In this ecumenical atmosphere, we have had the privilege of encountering people of all Christian denominations, and we have learned to worship God together. We have fellowship with people of all nationalities, and we have come to unity through the blood of Christ. Through chapel services, mission trips, community outreach, clubs, and organizations, we have learned to value each other as brothers and sisters. We are grateful for the relationships that have taught us to celebrate diversity. And yet, even with this lifeline, the question still resounds: Who wants to be a messenger, a messenger for God?

Finally, our last lifeline here at ORU has been the leadership of this campus. To Chancellor Oral Roberts and Mrs. Roberts, to President Richard Roberts and First Lady Roberts, to the Board of Regents, the Administration, and Staff: Thank you for your vision; Thank you for the seeds you have planted in our lives.

To the faculty, words cannot express our gratitude. Our eyes have been opened. Our ears have been loosed. Our hands have been freed in the classroom. You are the experts in your respective fields, yet you have chosen to teach here. You have chosen to teach us. Your words and your actions have brought us to the point where we can answer the question, Who wants to be a messenger, a messenger for God?

## A Seminary Dean's Experiment with Servant Leadership

With this last lifeline tapped, we must respond alone. Class of 2000, may our answer be: We choose to speak for God. We choose to bring healing to peoples' lives. We choose to be messengers—into the world of business, into the world of psychology, into the world of communications, into the world of theology, into the world of arts, into the world of education, into the world of music, into the world of nursing, into the world of science, into the world of engineering, into the world of drama, into the world of government, into every world!

Here we are, Lord, send us!

And yes, this is our final answer!

[The following is the transcribed text of my younger daughter Jamie's (Jamie Ann Mathew, JD, MBA) 2002 Valedictorian speech at ORU.]

## Oral Tradition

Solomon had to build a house for God. And all he had with him was the final blessing of his father David recorded in First Chronicles 28:20, "Be strong and courageous and do the work. Do not be afraid or discouraged, for the Lord, my God, is with you. He will not fail you or forsake you until all the work of the Lord is finished." Solomon carried an oral tradition. Solomon finished the temple.

We too have a job from God. David dreamed the temple. Solomon built it. Oral Roberts dreamed deliverance. We will spread it. We carry with us an Oral tradition.

We carry an Oral tradition of wholeness. The world has produced a number of good people: Gandhi, JFK, Mandela, Princess Diana. But these were not whole people. So does wholeness really matter then?

While 31.1 million Americans live in poverty, surviving on less than $90 a week, 800,000 people pay $90 a session to have acid peels put on their faces, so they can look younger. Consumers are paying up to $1395 to store their pets' genes until scientists learn how to clone their favorite cat or dog. And let us not forget John Wayne Gacy—building contractor, volunteer to hospital-ridden children, and rapist and murderer of 33 boys.

There is a Malayalam adage that says, "the boat must always be in the waters, but the waters must never be in the boat." We are surrounded by the waters of an unwholesome society, but our boat, protected by an Oral tradition, allowed none of it to seep in.

We have been through 41 final exams, two mottos, 256 chapels, eight field tests, swim proficiency test, and 2176 cafeteria meals. We have a unique understanding of wholeness, but we have not achieved this on our own. Bill Cosby once said to his kids, "I brought you into this world, and I can take you out." Thanks mom and dad for letting us stay. And to all our family members: thank you for supporting us. The class of 2002 thanks the administration, staff, and President and Mrs. Roberts for protecting the Oral tradition from compromise.

We like to thank the friends we made here. Through community outreach, academic societies, mission trips, Model United Nations, wing functions, and intramural, we have shared collective experiences. When our kids ask, where were you on September 11? We can say we were here, praying with friends. And most adamantly, (we like to) thank the faculty who have sacrificed the glory of their own profession so that we may be trained in ours. After completing 1950 contact hours with you, we have learned how to utilize our wholeness, for from wholeness comes healing. We carry an Oral tradition of healing.

The world thought healing had passed away when the last medical student walked across this stage, but healing has only begun! Fifty out of the 125 US medical schools are now teaching spirituality, claiming a subtle shift in the practice of medicine from treating a disease to treating a whole person. Sounds familiar? But disease is not just limited to the body. We are about to enter a world disintegrating from divorce, debt, pornography, prejudice, pollution, teen pregnancy, substance-abuse, suicide, and terrorism. Who will bring healing to this world gone awry?

Before the birth of Christ, the Roman empire called China *sares*, meaning silk, because the only knowledge it had of the Chinese empire came from the silk that had been sent to it. Likewise the world may not have the opportunity to come to Oral Roberts University, but we have been sent to it. And they will call us by our product. They will call us by our Oral tradition. They will call us healing.

Before we were born, Oral Roberts traveled the globe as a healing evangelist. To tens of thousands—black and white, rich and poor, male and female, he preached his Fourth Man sermon, and on one of these occasions, he so grievingly revealed, "I have the most unfinished ministry on earth. I think of my unfinished sermons. I think of my unfinished prayers, of the unfinished miracles, of the unfinished ministry of deliverance itself."

And so, I ask: Who will finish his ministry of deliverance? Who will carry his Oral tradition? We will. We will carry this Oral tradition—into universities, into businesses, into public schools, into hospitals, into art museums, into world politics, into laboratories, into equations, into court rooms, into nations, into theories, into the churches, into books, into theaters, into counseling centers, into philosophies, into music, into the hurting world so desperately seeking wholeness and healing.

We will preach the unpreached sermon. We will pray the un-prayed prayer. We will perform the unperformed miracle. For we are strong and courageous. And we will do the work. We are not afraid or discouraged, for the Lord God our God is with us. He will not fail us or forsake us, until all the work of the Lord is finished. We carry with us this Oral tradition.

If you believe it, say AMEN!

## ALSO BY THOMSON K. MATHEW

*Spirit-led Ministry in the Twenty-First Century*

*Spiritual Identity and Spirit-Empowered Life*

*Spiritual Identity and Spirit-Empowered Life Leader's Guide*

*What Will Your Tombstone Say?*

*Ministry Between Miracles*

*Ministry Research Simplified*

www.ingramcontent.com/pod-product-compliance
Lightning Source LLC
Chambersburg PA
CBHW030904080526
44589CB00010B/138